A Dirty Swindle

A Dirty Swindle

True Stories of Scots in the Great War

WALTER STEPHEN

Luath Press Limited

EDINBURGH

www.luath.co.uk

First published 2015

ISBN: 978-1-910745-13-7

The paper used in this book is recyclable. It is made from
low chlorine pulps produced in a low energy, low emissions manner
from renewable forests.

Printed and bound by
CPI Antony Rowe, Chippenham

Typeset in 11 point Sabon
by 3btype.com

Frontispiece 'Shell Shock!'
Anon – The Hydra

Contents

Introduction

True Stories

IN THE BOOK of Ecclesiastes, at Chapter 12, Verse 12 we read 'Of making many books there is no end: and much study is a weariness of the flesh'. In autumn 2013 the Prime Minister, David Cameron, rather gauchely announced that £60 million was to be spent on 'a celebration [of the First World War] that, like the Diamond Jubilee celebrations, says something about who we are as a people'. Since then, aided by Lord Ashcroft, the millionaire collector of Victoria Crosses, and the *Daily Telegraph*, there has been a steady flow of books and articles, films, plays and videos, about the war. Reminiscence has flowed and semi-forgotten and neglected monuments have been renovated or reinstated. This recent upwelling of interest in World War I is merely an upsurge in the process of retelling and analysing the story of that great struggle, a process which has gone on for almost a century, and which has produced some of the best work in literature and the visual arts.

Millions died in the Great War and millions more suffered catastrophic and irritating calamities. So, most of these True Stories are also Sad Stories; some beautifully expressed, some full of incoherent emotion. Do we need another 12?

John Keegan, in his masterly *The Face of Battle*, comments on the documentary sources for World War I:

> The regular battalions of the Guards and the regiments of the line added copiously to their existing histories... but humbler and more transient groups than these... at the peace vanished from public memory almost as quickly as they had been conjured into existence. It was not a deliberate act of obscuration. The regular regiments which had raised the greatest number of 'Service' battalions were often the least affluent (the rough rule of thumb in calculating the social status of an English regiment is that the further from London its depot, the less fashionable it will be, and the less monied its officers) and the least able therefore to stand the expense of printing a really exhaustive history.

So where does that leave the Scots? And can 'Keegan's Law' be applied to all aspects of the commemoration of World War 1?

On Wednesday 5 August 1914, the *Daily Telegraph*'s main headline was 'England's Declaration of War against Germany'.

What about Scotland? Is there nothing to be said about Wales, Ireland, Australia, Canada etc?

It is still a matter of extreme irritation to me that the bands in Whitehall insist on playing 'There'll Always Be An England' in the Armistice Day march-past. During the Second World War we used to sing:

There'll always be an England,
As long as Scotland's there,
To do the work
And share the care.

Penguin Books republished *Poems of the Great War* in 2014; 145 pages of excellent, moving poetry. Three poems were by women. None by Scots. (John McCrae – 'In Flanders fields the poppies blow/ Between the crosses, row on row' – despite the name, was Canadian). So we miss, for example, 'the sheer awfulness and horror of war... simply but impressively portrayed... in the touching litany of *The Glen's Muster Roll: The Dominie Loquitur*' by Mary Symon – which supplies the emotion which parallels my observations on the quiet places in the chapter 'Memento Mori'. This is not conscious discrimination, it is merely a consequence of the relationship between Scotland and its great neighbour, described by Andrew Fletcher of Saltoun (1655–1716) as being 'in bed with an elephant'.

First World War Poets by Alan Judd and David Crane is, as one would expect from one of the National Portrait Gallery Companions series, an excellent little book. Unusually, each of the 17 poets is given his military rank and dates before a short essay recounts his life (and, too often, his death). Thus we have Captain Hon. Julian Grenfell DSO (1888–1915). Each one has his portrait or photograph, almost always showing them at their best. Then comes one of his poems. (To be pedantic, only 15 are military, one was a civil servant and Lawrence Binyon – 'They shall not grow old, as we that are left grow old' – served at the Front with the Red Cross.) And not a Scot among them, the nearest being Second Lieutenant

AA Milne, creator of Winnie the Pooh 'and the least military soldier imaginable', whose father was a Scot who moved to London.

There may be a problem of class. In a big article in the *Sunday Telegraph* ('The Path from Playing Fields to Flanders Fields') Jeremy Paxman looks at 'the vital role schools and their pupils played in the First World War':

> He points out that more than 1,000 Etonians never returned from the war, and... that there can hardly have been a school in the country that did not send its own contingent of young men to perish, including nearly 700 from Rugby and Cheltenham... from Winchester... and 450 from other second-division public schools such as Malvern and Uppingham.

'Headmasters... were broken', but there is no reference, for example, to the likes of Mary Symon's country headmaster mentioned above. Are we to imagine that the bulk of the 20,000 killed on 1 July 1916 did not attend school? Twenty senior students from Broughton Higher Grade School in Edinburgh were led in to McCrae's Battalion by their bespectacled mathematics teacher Peter Ross. Were there others like that? Nor does Paxman mention that the high death rate among young officers was not due to chance, but by their being distinctively accoutred and armed. Thus, enemy snipers were able to take out the officers first, leaving the squaddies leaderless and in confusion.

Sir Hew Strachan, Chichele Professor of the History of War, Fellow at All Souls College, Oxford and a member of the World War 1 Centenary Advisory Board, has similar anxieties. He maintains that the educational ambition behind the centenary is not being met and that we are being presented with 'a British war and one fought almost exclusively against Germany'. Local projects have stimulated local interests 'but they hardly match the war's scale' and, for example, in setting up 'Engagement Centres':

> Not even a national spread has been achieved, as the most northerly of the recipients is Nottingham, and, while Northern Ireland is covered, Wales and Scotland are not.

While I agree with Sir Hew and am conscious that these True Stories are essentially local and small-scale, I think it will be clear that there are bigger issues raised in most of them. And, as Martin Luther said when he protested against the evils of the Church – 'I can do no other!'

Although I have never fired a shot in anger, I could be described as a trained professional killer and as having some understanding of the military mind. Thousands of us, still alive, are criticised for creating a pensions crisis by living too long. Yet we gave up two years of our lives in the National Service of our country while others, of poor health, or in supposedly valuable occupations, or in Northern Ireland, stayed at home and built themselves nice little careers, thank you. For the first 16 weeks of basic training we were paid four shillings (20 pence) a day, although this increased with service, additional qualifications and, perhaps, promotion. Bed, board and uniform were provided, but for those fortunate enough to be commissioned, a tailor and a hatter came down from London to fit us for our service dress and mess dress, for which we had to pay.

Almost all of the regulars at that time had served in the Second World War and a glance at their medal ribbons told one what they had been up to. Or rather, where they had been. For example, the Burma Star was awarded for service in Burma between certain dates, or in Bengal or Assam between certain other dates, or in China or Malaya between other dates. But they give no indication of the quality of service!

Everyone had the Defence Medal and the War Medal. A chap with the Africa Star would have a clasp with an '8' for Eighth Army, or a '1' for the First Army, and an Italy Star, and a France and Germany Star. In 1952–54 there was fighting in Korea and in Malaya, and fresh ribbons from these campaigns were much in evidence. Those who had been in Korea had two medals: the British Korea Medal and the United Nations Korea Service Medal.

The Victoria Cross and the Military Cross will come up again. I served under two captains who wore the ribbon for the MC. They were both small, vital men who contrived to be enthusiastic in their dull peacetime roles. For 13 Command Workshops, REME – a huge garage in uniform – one was the scrum half in the Rugby team. He and I (in the forwards) were the pillars of the team but this did not diminish his occasional justified criticisms of the performance of my duties. The other was assiduous in trying to persuade me to 'sign on' as a regular.

Captain Stagg, Royal Artillery, who had just returned from Korea, was the Chief Instructor of my section at Mons Officer Cadet School. On manoeuvres, when it was my turn to command the section, he was kind enough to say that my leadership would have earned me the MC in action.

Very gratifying, but one wonders just how one would have behaved if the situation had been real and 'the guns began to roar'.

The initial basic training of 16 weeks was fairly strenuous, rather noisy, but confidence-building for most. There was hectoring and some bullying. There were 'accidents' on the rifle range. Some fellows tried to 'work their ticket', trying to get discharged on account of poor health, psychological unsuitability or by shooting themselves in the foot – an offence 'punishable by death or any less penalty that the court martial may impose'. There was the occasional suicide. I spent a rather enjoyable period jaunting round Britain and bringing back prisoners – mostly poor souls who had overstayed their leave (usually because of some girl) and had been picked up by the police. Very romantic and dramatic on the stage in Bizet's *Carmen*, but all very pathetic in real life.

The regimental depot where the trained soldiers waited till they were posted to their units was not a happy place. A wee corporal of the Seaforth Highlanders supplemented his pay by soliciting backhanders from those wanting a nice posting near home, and certainly not in the Empire's hotspots. In 1952 there was still rationing and many a seven-pound tin of ham found its way from the cookhouse or the stores to the town.

'Those bloody Jocks' had their value in Aldershot. Before the motorway network was built, a fleet of coaches would pick up hundreds of troops at tea-time on Friday and hurry them off to places like Leicester, Birmingham and Manchester. From Sunday night at midnight they would bring back the unhappy weekenders, who proceeded to spend most of Monday sleeping on whatever job they were supposed to be doing. The Jocks were useful in that they could look after the shop, releasing these others for their 36- and 48-hour passes, for certain favours. On the weekend of the Coronation, the entire British Army was either lining the route or off on leave, and I really believe that, in Aldershot at least, the only people on duty were an elderly major in the Royal Pavilion (who had no home to go to) and myself!

Once they got to their units, many of the technical squaddies settled into jobs not too unlike those they might have been doing in 'civvy' street (the infantry and cavalry were different) and it was a question of serving out one's time without too much trouble to oneself or to others – 'one day more, one day less.' 'Roll on demob.' Grumbling and a sense of humour were the two safety valves which kept the bulk of the armed services going.

Do these snapshots of military life in the 1950s shed any light at all on what it was like to serve in World War I? The first shock of war was borne by the regulars and territorials. Then came the troops from the Empire (not the Commonwealth) and the volunteers, like Kitchener's 'First Hundred Thousand' and the 'Pals battalions'. But by 1916 the pot of enthusiasm had been scraped bare, and it was conscription that filled the gaps and created the force that eventually wore the enemy down. In my time the armed services were vast and complex, headed up and led by regulars, almost all of whom had served in World War II, and had been decorated accordingly. But they were clearly not all heroes and it is facilely sentimental to suppose that all those who fought and died in World War I were heroes as well.

We were spared two unsettling uncertainties. It was most unlikely that many of us would be killed, while most of our Great War equivalents would see action – and its consequences. We also knew how long we were going to serve (although at one point National Service doctors were not allowed to be demobilised because they could not be replaced). It was clear by the end of August 1914 that the war would not be over by Christmas and every year had its 'big push' – Loos in 1915, the Somme in 1916, Passchendaele in 1917 – after each of which there was still 'a long, long trail a-winding'. When the Germans broke through in early 1918 it must have seemed that the war would never end.

The traditionalists object to *Oh! What a Lovely War*, *Blackadder* and some of the war poetry as being defeatist, unpatriotic and disrespectful of the dead. I think they miss the point – which is that it is, as I said earlier, through grumbling, through little acts disrespectful of authority and, above all, through humour, that ordinary folk cope with the realities of war.

I sometimes have anxieties about what might be called the cult of the Victoria Cross. As George MacDonald Fraser puts it in *The General Danced at Dawn*:

> There are... 'good VCs' and ordinary VCs – so far as winning the VC can ever be called ordinary... I imagine if it were possible to take a poll of the most famous VCs over the past century Piper George Findlater would be challenging for the top spot... what he did on an Afghan hillside one afternoon caught the public imagination, as it deserved to, more than such things commonly do.

The pipe-sergeant recounts:

The pipers was out in front – as usual – and Findlater was shot through first one ankle then through the other, and fell among the rocks in front of the Afghan positions. And he pulled himself up, and crawled to his pipes, and him pourin' bleed, and got himself up on a rock wi' the shots pingin' away round him, and played the regimental march so that the boys took heart and carried the crest.

What made Findlater's deed special was not just his personal courage but the fact that attacks earlier in the day by county regiments and the Gurkhas had been repulsed, but the Gordons had been so encouraged by the 'Cock o' the North' that they succeeded where the others had failed.

The Heights of Dargai caught the public imagination. Pictures were painted and prints made. 'Cock o' the North' was sounded up the length and breadth of the land, in music-halls, and by brass bands, and by street fiddlers. The butcher boys in the street whistled it and sang it to naughty words. The Queen travelled down to Netley Hospital in Hampshire to pin the VC on the hero.

I feel a certain relationship with Findlater and his great deed. My grandfather was one of the heroes that day and met Findlater later, after South Africa. In Edinburgh, in 1947, my pal Eddy Wilson would go up to the top flat and take down the ash-bucket of Findlater's sisters. Under it there was always a shiny new penny.

But there were other VCs won that day on the Heights of Dargai. Private Lawson (an Englishman in the Gordons):

Carried Lieutenant Dingwall (who was wounded and unable to move), out of a heavy fire, and subsequently returned and brought in Private McMillan, being himself wounded in two places.

When an officer of:

The Derbyshire Regiment was struck down, Lieutenant Pennell ran to his assistance and made two attempts, under a hail of bullets, to carry and drag him back to cover. The Lieutenant only gave up when he found that the wounded officer was dead.

Private Vickery of the Dorsetshires:

Ran down the slope and rescued a wounded comrade under heavy fire, bringing him back to cover.

Findlater is remembered, the others not. Why? Findlater was a 'good' VC because he not only showed courage, but his actions influenced (or were believed to have influenced) the course of the engagement. For the others, it is very important for morale to know that the wounded will not be left to die out there between the lines, and therefore those who bring them in are carrying out a constructive and humane act in a general sense, but are probably not achieving the military objectives of the action in any way. Sassoon probably had his tongue in his cheek when he said of the action for which he received his MC:

> It was only the sort of thing which people often did during a fire or a railway accident.

We can see what he means.

The *Sunday Telegraph* devoted two pages, with photographs, to Private George Peachment (18) who, after a failed attack in the Battle of Loos, 'Showing great bravery... went to the aid of his officer who had been seriously wounded'. The citation for the medal said:

> He knelt in the open by his officer and tried to help him, but while doing this he was first wounded by a bomb and a minute later mortally wounded by a rifle bullet. He was one of the youngest men in his battalion, and gave this splendid example of courage and self-sacrifice.

His officer, Captain Guy Dubs, survived (someone else must have brought him in) and recommended Peachment for the VC. He wrote twice to Mrs Peachment saying to her that he had made George his orderly just before the battle in an attempt to prevent him having to go over the top. He confessed:

> I am afraid I feel very responsible for his death, because I might have sent him home a short time before when I found out his age, only he was so keen to stay.

I wonder if I am alone in feeling that, amid all the terror and courage of battle, where scenes like this must have been replicated many times, there is something uncomfortable in this award and in Michael Ashcroft's title for his article – 'No man could have been braver'.

In the Lewis Grassic Gibbon Centre in Arbuthnott there is an interesting little display referring to Lance Corporal Robert Walker of the 1st Gordon Highlanders. On 26 August 1914 he carried a wounded comrade called Addlestone for three miles behind the German lines. On 13 October he was shot in the head by the enemy and died in St Mark's College Hospital in London on 25 October. In a glass case are his three standard

World War I medals, the 'Widow's Penny', and a very attractive Médaille Militaire. A framed certificate from the President of France records that Walker had been awarded the Médaille Militaire for his courage in action. Odd, isn't it?

From the Great War, Zeebrugge is an interesting case study. Early in 1918 the U-boat campaign had brought Britain almost to its knees, and it was decided that the Flanders flotilla of the Imperial German Navy should be locked into its Zeebrugge base. My *Pageant of the Century* of 1933 covers the raid in four pages, with 11 photographs. It says:

> Admiral Sir Roger Keyes was the executive to whom the Zeebrugge operation was entrusted. With consummate skill he succeeded in sinking the vessels designated to form the block inside the Mole... and a landing party did magnificent work on the Mole... [German] headquarters staff officers rushed to Zeebrugge to direct the defence against the British attack, but the precision with which the carefully drawn plans were carried out rendered all German efforts abortive.

In part nine of the *Sunday Telegraph's* 'Inside the First World War' series, a double page is devoted to Zeebrugge. When the attack came, on 22 April, it was at the fourth attempt, 'as the weather and wind direction had conspired against us'. 'The events of that night were dramatic and, at times, confused'. An old cruiser, HMS *Vindictive*, and two old Mersey ferry boats were sunk – but in the wrong place – and a storming party of Royal Marines landed on the Mole. A parallel attack was made on Ostend, but was called off.

The canal was opened up again after two days. The British suffered 227 dead and 356 wounded. German losses were eight dead and 16 wounded.

The British suffered 47 casualties at Ostend compared with just 11 for the enemy. There is no doubt, however, that there were many cases of incredible bravery by individuals and the raid resulted in the award of three VCs and numerous other gallantry awards.

And eight VCs were awarded for Zeebrugge.

How can we strike a balance sheet for Zeebrugge? On the one hand, 600 casualties for a very temporary advantage. On the other, 11 examples of heroic behaviour in the hurly-burly of war.

A Dirty Swindle: True Stories of the Great War is not an attack on Mr Cameron, Lord Ashworth and the *Daily Telegraph*. The Great War, as we called it in my young days, was clearly such a cataclysmic event that everyone should know about it and its effects – on the world, not just Britain. It is good that the public should be reminded and informed about events, that communities and individuals be involved in research and commemoration, and that what arose out of the ashes of war be considered. But the task is vast and there is a need for the occasional qualification or redirection. So *A Dirty Swindle* is unashamedly Scottish, and homes in on some interesting angles which are often ignored or forgotten in the face of the major tragedy.

Siegfried Sassoon knew a thing or two about the Great War, and it was he who described it as 'a dirty swindle'. In *King Richard II* Shakespeare writes:

> For God's sake, let us sit upon the ground
> And tell sad stories of the death of kings:
> How some have been depos'd, some slain in war,
> Some haunted by the ghosts they have depos'd,
> Some poison'd by their wives, some sleeping kill'd;
> All murdered.

There follow True Stories aplenty, of subjects of kings and emperors, slain in war and in a variety of different ways. Some poisoned by gas, some killed while they slept. And there are ghosts and nightmares. Were they all murdered? Or did they give up their lives willingly? Impossible to give one answer that fits all. No attempt is made to milk the misery of war, the facts are miserable enough as they stand.

And yet the last two True Stories remind us of the complexities of the great conflict and the resilience of the human spirit in coming through the most frightful experiences. Here is an overview of the themes explored in this book, chapter by chapter.

'A Peace Warrior and His Family in the Great War' is centred around Patrick Geddes (1854–1932), 'a most unsettling person', a world figure who has been summarised as 'Biologist, Town Planner, Re-educator, Peace-warrior'. He and six members of his family were involved in the Great War, were affected by it and tried to do something about preventing it, winning it or mitigating its worst effects. They are of interest because each member played a distinctive role – if minor – in the great drama that was played out across the world.

'Out of the Frying Pan' is the saddest of stories, of the 1/7th (Leith) Battalion of the Royal Scots, whose troop train from Larbert to Liverpool (for Gallipoli) crashed at speed and went on fire at Quintinshill, near Gretna, in Britain's worst train accident. The survivors were scraped together and with numbers made up from other units formed the 4th and 7th Royal Scots. In Gallipoli, 37 days after the rail disaster, they took part in a massive and costly attack on the Turkish positions. A further horror has to be recorded. The Mediterranean scrub and grass was set on fire and swept across no-man's land, where the poor wounded suffered a horrible death within earshot of their comrades. Some had survived the frying pan of Quintinshill only to be consumed in the fire of Gallipoli.

'Dark Lochnagar' takes its title from a big mountain in Aberdeenshire, visible from a great distance and with great sentimental associations. Byron celebrated it in poetry, Queen Victoria climbed it. On the first day of the Somme, the Lochnagar Mine(s) failed to make the advance of McCrae's Battalion an easy stroll. In St Giles Cathedral, Edinburgh, in 1923, at the unveiling of the memorial to McCrae's Battalion, Pipe Major Willie Duguid piped up Dark Lochnagar.

The beauty of the winter solitude of Lochnagar contrasts so strongly with the sordid reality of 'Man's inhumanity to man'.

The next three chapters form a kind of triptych in that they each derive mainly from a book, but each subject is dealt with in its own style. The individual narratives are interesting, but considered together they raise questions about truth, the nature of evidence and the appropriate style for reminiscence.

'The First Hundred Thousand' takes its title from a book by 'Ian Hay', the nom de plume of Captain Beith, describing the recruiting, training and first major action of a fictional Highland regiment (based on the Argyll and Sutherland Highlanders, in which the author served). It is straight-forward and displays the qualities of grumbling and humour I have praised earlier.

It concludes with the Battle of Loos, which began on 25 September 1915. (In 'real life' Beith made it to Major, won the Military Cross at Loos – not mentioned in the book – and was Mentioned in Dispatches.) The book was a publishing tour de force in that it came out before the end of 1915. Much of it must have been written 'on the hoof' and in the trenches and, as evidence, must rank very highly in terms of truth. Today's literati may consider it trivial and naïve, but his final message is loyal and optimistic, but prophetic. Hay's voice must be respected for its immediacy.

'McCrae's – Eponymous or Anonymous?' tells the story of Sir George

McCrae's rise from obscurity to success as a businessman and politician, and of the 16th Battalion of the Royal Scots, a Service Battalion which was raised and led by the charismatic McCrae.

Around 1990 one Jack Alexander found that virtually all the battalion's records had been destroyed. None of Edinburgh's many museums, libraries or archives seemed to hold a single item. Fortunate that some survivors were still alive, he worked for 12 years to produce probably the best record there is of a Service Battalion – *McCrae's Battalion: The Story of the 16th Royal Scots*. From documents, letters, photographs and interviews he built up a readable history of scholarly quality.

The contrast in approach with *The First Hundred Thousand* could hardly be greater, but both rank highly in terms of integrity and honesty. Alexander must have been pleased that McCrae's Battalion was rescued from anonymity by Jeremy Paxman, who devoted a ten minute slot in one of his World War I programmes to the recruiting of McCrae's and the example set by the Hearts footballers.

'The War Poets in the Eye of the Storm' focuses on the best-known War Poets, Siegfried Sassoon and Wilfred Owen, who each spent several months in the Slateford Military Hospital for shell-shocked officers in Edinburgh. Much of what we know about this important encounter comes from Siegfried Sassoon who, after a decade or so of poetry, published *Memoirs of a Fox-Hunting Man*, which won the 1928 James Tait Black Award for fiction. Yes, fiction. In 1930 *Memoirs of an Infantry Officer* followed, then *Sherston's Progress* in 1936. The three books were published together in 1937 as *The Complete Memoirs of George Sherston*. George Sherston is, of course, a thinly disguised Sassoon and his trilogy is a beautifully written account of how he came to be in Craiglockhart, what it was like to be there and what happened after.

A comparison of the three books is a fascinating task. Ian Hay's book is fresh, but perhaps too conformist and optimistic for some. Sassoon is describing events of more than ten years before, and memory is notoriously unreliable and selective, while Jack Alexander has no experience of war against which to measure the testimony of his subjects.

'Memento Mori' is a thoughtful chapter devoted to the examination of war memorials; particularly in the rural and remote corners of Scotland, where the death toll was high, and one feels the losses hastened depopulation and the emptying of the glens.

'Their Name Liveth…' describes how I stumbled across two military cemeteries on opposite sides of Edinburgh. Each was associated with a nearby military hospital. One is exemplary in its neatness, maintenance and discreet information, while the other is neglected, with the stones all awry and the ground unkempt. In one, the True Stories may be mitigated a little by the respectful treatment of the dead. In the other, one smiles cynically at the inscription 'Their Name Liveth for Ever' and muses on the difference between public recognition and private forgetfulness.

'Observe the Sons of Ulster…' takes us to Londonderry in Northern Ireland, a city with strong links to Scotland, where, in 2008, long before Mr Cameron, Lord Ashcroft and the *Daily Telegraph,* the Diamond War Memorial Project researched and published information on the 756 individuals from the city whose names are recorded on the Diamond War Memorial.

Given the political climate in Ireland in 1916, many Ulstermen, fearful of reprisals to their loved ones, crossed the North Channel to enlist in Scottish regiments. The First of July was already a special day, a day full of symbols, songs and slogans for the Sons of Ulster. Thus, in Northern Ireland, the first day of the Battle of the Somme acquired an especial significance, as on that day the Ulster Division incurred fearful losses while doing better than most.

'The Scottish National War Memorial' looks at the memorial situated on the highest point of the Edinburgh Castle Rock, an old Army barrack turned into a dignified national monument and shrine devoted to those who died for their country in the Great War. (Subsequent conflicts have been unobtrusively recognised.)

Visited by crowds of camera-carrying tourists of all nations, it still invokes an atmosphere of respect and bewilderment at the terrible scale of the losses commemorated there and the vast complexity of modern war. There is no triumphalism, only perhaps a perfectly understandable idealism of those who served and the cause for which they died.

The last two chapters are True Stories, revealing that, in the midst of sadness, there is still some good to be found.

'God bless the Kaiser' reminds us that, amid all the death and destruction and while every community had its losses, for some the Great War brought much-needed benefits. 'Now thrive the armourers' says The Prologue in *Henry V* and, of course, the war profiteers did very nicely and picked up substantial rewards, both financial and in honours from a grateful nation. Isaac Rosenberg – whom some consider as the finest of the War Poets – returned from South Africa and enlisted in 1915. 'His main concern was for the parlous finances of his family'. He was probably not the only one. The war brought food shortages and high prices, so that small ports with their inshore fisheries received a welcome boost to their dying activities. Part of the sadness is that we had to have a war for these things to happen and that 'the land fit for heroes' failed to materialise.

Field Marshal Haig has been vilified for having been an insensitive butcher who sent the youth of the nation to their deaths, a polo-playing buffoon out of touch with the reality of war and those who fought in it, a conservative leader resistant to and unable to change.

'Andra and the Field-Marshal' is a post-war snapshot which reveals that Haig had more to him than the highly-polished boots of the cavalry-man. More than that, it reveals that Haig – and presumably many more – had a resilience that helped him to set aside the terrible traumas of conflict.

Emotion does not shine through these True Stories. One thinks back to the spring of 2010, when the eruption of a fairly small volcano in Iceland caused a volcanic ash cloud which affected most of Europe and perhaps 10,000,000 air passengers. One recalls the scenes at Glasgow Airport with irritated and harassed passengers. And one recalls one Glasgow man, with his trolley piled high with luggage, saying – 'You cannae be angry wi' a volcano.' It's too big and completely beyond our control. Similarly, it could be said that you cannot be angry about the Great War. It's too big, it was always beyond control and, anyway, it was a long time ago and far away.

Nevertheless, there is emotion in the writing of these True Stories. One cannot compete with the imagination of Pat Barker or the clever irony of *Oh What a Lovely War!* But one can certainly feel the anger at the inhumanity of someone like 'Hunter-Bunter' – who sent the Royal Scots' survivors from the Gretna disaster into the hell of Gallipoli just 37 days later, and did almost the same thing, but on a bigger scale, the following year in Flanders – and contempt for the sustained dishonesty and lack of supervision of the railwaymen responsible for the disaster. One almost weeps at the thought of Mrs McClay asking Daisy McBride's mother to sit with her on the anniversary of the day her three sons were killed. Or the rage at the old men, and especially the despot Franz Josef, who had the power to use other means to resolve their jealousies and had not the wit or care for their subjects to do so. Or sense the perplexity of the ageing Peace Warrior grieving for his son, proud of his achievement, yet unable to break the news to the dying mother.

Mary Symon's dominie concludes his soliloquy:

For every lauchin' loon I kent I see a hell-scarred man.
Not mine but yours to question now! You lift unhappy eyes –
'Ah, Maister, tell's fat a' this means.' And I, ye thocht sae wise,
Maun answer wi' the bairn words ye said to me langsyne:
'I dinna ken, I dinna ken.' Fa does, oh, Loons o' Mine?

Are we any the wiser today?

CHAPTER I

A Peace Warrior and His Family in the Great War

THE NUMBER SEVEN has a mystical, even religious, aura. There are seven days in a week. There were Seven Wonders in the Ancient World. There were seven senses, Seven Deadly Sins and Seven Virtues. There were Seven Champions of Christendom, perhaps reincarnated in our own time as The Magnificent Seven. In south Germany the Seven Gallant Swabians still do stupid things. And Patrick Geddes and six members of his family were involved in the Great War, were affected by it and tried to do something about preventing it, winning it or mitigating its worst effects.

This was an unusual family. It was not a representative sample nor a statistical cross-section of the nation at the time, but it is of interest for that very reason, and because each member played a distinctive role – if minor – in the great drama that was played out across the world.

Patrick Geddes (1854–1932)

Patrick Geddes was 'a most unsettling person'. He has been summarised as 'Biologist, Town Planner, Re-educator, Peace Warrior'. He described himself as 'the little boy who rings the bell and runs away'. Some idea of the breadth and richness of Geddes's life will be gained from the Appendix – Extract from *Who's Who* 1930. Born in Ballater, he grew up in Perth and went on to national and international fame. His mantra 'Think Global, Act Local' (*Cities in Evolution,* 1917) has become the conventional wisdom of our time.

How and from whom does a Peace Warrior acquire his beliefs?

Patrick Geddes's father was a professional soldier who served in the ranks of the 42nd Foot (Black Watch) for 21 years and 304 days before being discharged 'having been found unfit for further service, as per Medical Officer's Certificate'. His general character was 'very good' and he was headhunted for 'special duties' at Balmoral, then being renovated for Victoria and Albert. In February 1855 he was commissioned into the

Perthshire Militia, first as Ensign, then Lieutenant and Quartermaster. His service as an officer totalled 23 years and 37 days – not bad for one who had 'been found unfit for further service, as per Medical Officer's Certificate' in 1851!

Alexander Geddes served at home (which then included Ireland) and in Corfu, Malta and Bermuda. It is unlikely that, in 44-plus years of service, he ever heard a shot fired in anger. So, Patrick Geddes grew up in a home with God-fearing parents and an atmosphere of discipline and control – but with no gory reminiscences of war and battle. Although for almost 20 years his father must have spent the daylight hours in uniform, in Geddes's reminiscences of growing up it was the arts of peace – reliability, growing things, observing the natural landscape – which he admired and acquired from his parents.

Yet it was not all totally serious and in the family correspondence there is also humour, often expressed as rather ponderous semi-military banter. Brother Jack from New Zealand writes to: 'The Detachment of the "None Duck"', invoking himself 'and the other Authorities at Head Qrs', hoping 'the wounded are progressing' and 'enclosing Despatches... from Mexico'. He addresses his father as 'you and your Dept Assistant Adjt General... on the sick list', and is 'glad to see the Pay Master General has given' (his sister Jessie) 'a small allowance of pocket money'. And there was remembered belligerence, as when Jack wrote,

> Knowing my motto would ever be the same as Pat's when he used to go forth to slay the dockens at the Pig's sty 'Victory or death'.

An original approach to violence was demonstrated by Geddes in 1879, when he was on a collecting trip for the British Association. Mexico was in turmoil and Robert Geddes (Patrick's banking brother)

> Tried to make his brother carry a revolver when he rode out of the city to look for specimens, since bandits were by no means uncommon. Geddes, however, preferred to carry £5 for possible ransom money, and planned hopefully to rely on his prowess at la boxe francaise if captured.

In the 1880s Geddes was commissioned to write articles for the *Encyclopaedia Britannica* and *Chambers' Encyclopaedia*. In articles on Darwin, *Darwinian Theory and Evolution*, and in his book *The Evolution of Sex*, he reinforced and clarified the evidence for evolution by natural selection. However, he took issue with Huxley and his well-known assertion that:

> From the point of view of the naturalist the world is on about the same level as a gladiator's show.

Geddes had doubts about 'survival of the fittest' – Herbert Spencer's coinage replacing 'natural selection' – and Tennyson's 'Nature red in tooth and claw' from *In Memoriam*. *The Evolution of Sex* suggests that:

> As well as struggle, cruelty and selfishness in evolution, there is also cooperation; and that 'creation's final law' is not struggle but love.

In the Chambers' 'Evolution' entry, examples were produced suggesting that 'evolution is primarily a materialised ethical process'. With moral optimism Geddes concluded that:

> It is possible to interpret the ideals of ethical progress – through love and sociality, co-operation and sacrifice, not as mere utopias contradicted by experience, but as the highest expressions of the central evolutionary process of the natural world.

For the *Encyclopaedia Britannica* Geddes provided an article on *Variation and Selection*. After lengthy coverage of the Laws of Variation, Geddes concluded by repeating that competition in nature and organic progress are not necessarily cause and effect, and suggests that environmental and social factors also play their part:

> The ideal of Evolution is thus an Eden; and, although competition can never be wholly eliminated... it is much for our pure natural history to see no longer struggle, but love, as creation's final law.

> While ceasing to speak of indefinite variation we may of course still conveniently retain the rest of the established phraseology and continue to speak of 'natural selection' and of 'survival of the fittest', always provided that... we make the transition from the self-regarding to the other-regarding.

(There are occasions when Geddes seems to be deliberately trying to be difficult. 'Self-regarding' is the struggle for life, the survival of the fittest, while 'other-regarding'– love – was 'creation's final law'.)

One might suppose that this optimistic view could only have been shaken by the First World War, but on the death of Geddes in 1932, SA Robertson, a former student at Geddes's *Collége des Ecossais*, paid *A Scottish Tribute*:

> Even a noble soul like Huxley could see in life essentially a 'gladiator's show'. Geddes... challenged the verdict in his books, in his lectures, in

the flood of vivacious speech which leaped from him like a fountain. I recall the thrill which went through an audience as he traced the basal feature of all life to be the sacrifice of the mother for her offspring and closed by saying... 'So life is not really a gladiator's show; it is rather – a vast mothers' meeting!'

Most historians seem to agree that the Great War was the result of the Great Powers 'sleepwalking into Armageddon', and that there was an inevitability about the process that the great ones of Europe were unable to do anything about. The appropriate section of the Imperial War Museum is dominated by a relentless ticking clock, counting down to August 1914 – or is it the ticking of a time bomb about to explode?

Some of the factors which, in succession, seemed to create this mood of urgency and tension are listed below – in increasing order of tension:

- The formation of Imperial Germany in 1872
- French desire for revenge and the return of Alsace and Lorraine
- 'The Scramble for Africa' and the acquisition of colonies
- The crumbling of the Ottoman empire and Balkanisation
- Massive industrialisation and innovation, but not at a uniform pace
- The arms race (eg Dreadnoughts from 1906)
- Orchestrated xenophobia and jingoism

Given unprecedented investment by governments in such ventures, war must have seemed inevitable and even desirable, but there were those who thought otherwise. Around 1900 there were over 400 Peace Societies in US and Europe. There were two International Peace Conferences in The Hague and in 1906 Andrew Carnegie, the Scot who said 'The man who dies rich is... disgraced' came up with $1.5 million to build the Peace Palace, officially opened on 28 August 1913.

In 1897 Geddes and his wife spent three months in Cyprus, whose economy was in a state of collapse, dragged down further by 10,000 Armenian refugees. Using his Planning Model (Sympathy, Synthesis, Synergy or Survey, Plan, Action) he fundamentally examined the problems – most a consequence of the long-term degradation of habitat common to most Mediterranean societies – and came up (in 1,000 pages) with a rehabilitation programme. An excellent and inspiring document, which was to be the basis for a life's work, but too radical for the politicians and the colonial authorities.

During the First World War Geddes used his Summer Meetings to organise his thoughts on 'Wardom' and 'Peacedom', published as a 20-page article in the *Sociological Review*. He saw the war as the logical outcome of 19th century Darwinism. British and German minds were dazzled by the 'impressive nature-myth' of tooth-and-claw competition which Darwin and his followers mainly saw in organic evolution. The whole trend of natural science and politics for half a century was based on half-truths and guided by colossal errors of interpretation. Darwin had read nature largely in terms of industrial conflict, of economic survival of the fittest, and in turn, the industrialists and economists found in Darwin's projection of their system upon nature the justification for continuing in their ways. German scientists and Prussian imperialists then went all out in adapting this British-industrial conception of evolution to their *Kultur* and their goal of world-dominion. And since 1914 the Prussian statecraft of brute force had openly been hurling this Darwinism of 'might is right' back at the Allies.

This last paragraph is decidedly sharper than his earlier, academic, thoughts. Why was this? The answer lies in one word – Louvain.

Louvain is an ancient university city 15 miles east of Brussels. Traditionally the rules of warfare held that war was only lawful if it was conducted between armies of uniformed soldiers. A civilised country does not wage war on the civilian population. There has always been a problem with guerrilla warfare, where uniformed troops are attacked by loosely organised armed civilians.

In August 1914 the German army took most of Belgium easily, and the occupation began fairly smoothly. There were incidents when Belgian civilians destroyed bridges and there were civilian snipers, but the occupying forces reacted with paranoia and allegations that this partisan activity was being organised 'from above'. Hostages were taken, and sometimes shot, men and boys were deported to Germany. Villages and towns were pillaged and burnt. For six days Louvain was burnt, including the ancient library of 1426 with its 230,000 volumes. Civilians were shot. On 29 August highly-coloured reports appeared in the foreign press and on 30 August the process of destroying Louvain as an example to others stopped.

But the image of Germany had been irrevocably changed from the 'fat old bandmaster with a string of sausages hanging out of his pocket'. Romain Rolland asked, 'Are you descendants of Goethe or Attila the

Hun?' English headlines proclaimed 'The March of the Hun' and 'Treason to Civilisation'. For many the war had changed from a power struggle between nations to a fight against barbarism. For Geddes his stance against militarism had been mainly intellectual. Now it had an element of compassion and outrage on behalf of the victims of militarism.

Before moving on to the outbreak of the Great War, it must be noted that Geddes had a certain regard, probably rather romanticised and idealised, for things military. He took pride in his family association with loyalty and responsibility, and saw the Scottish soldier in a tradition of service to worthy causes. A favourite example was the Scots bodyguard to Joan of Arc in her struggle for freedom from English domination.

Geddes had no ear for music, but had a great attachment to the Great Highland Bagpipe, not because of the beauties of its 'very extraordinary scale', but because of its historical and cultural importance. Thus we find him writing to Alasdair, then 13, in 1904:

> You have always worn the costume of our Highland forbears, as I did as a boy, my father as a man, but we have both lost their language. Learn then this wider language, that by which the Celt at once appeals to every Scottish ear. Learn to play the old Celtic laments, the marches too, the pibrochs: blow loud and clear till men think of the long-lost Arthur returning in his might; croon too with the doves of peace; and chant like Columba and his brethren.
>
> In a summer or two you will lead some of our excursions, and almost from the first you will be able to start the march and help the fun.

Later, he writes:

> Though in Edinburgh we have made great pageants, we can do wonders with but a single piper. For children cannot but follow; the procession thus soon forms, and grows. All passers-by become spectators, and faces come to windows, soon opening down the long unlovely street. Better too than him of Hamelin, our piper leads to some new Children's Garden, henceforth their own for work and play. The music passes, yet even as things are, in this 'day of small things', its sowing of citizenship is not all lost.

And in the Strathclyde University Archive is an appallingly bad photograph showing Alasdair leading the children of Castlehill School down to their new garden.

Lady Aberdeen, twice Vicereine of Ireland, was a vigorous and masterful force for good, who enlisted the support of Geddes in her attempts to transform Ireland through public health provision and enlightened urban planning. They were two strong personalities, who both regarded a successful exhibition as an essential first stage in implementing changes in a city, which had all the problems of a major British city as well as being a focus for national unrest.

In early summer, 1911, Geddes's *Cities and Town Planning Exhibition* was held in Dublin and was followed up by a development plan and programme of activities.

At the meeting of the Housing and Town Planning Association in January 1914, the President (Lady Aberdeen) informed them that they were going to stage a Civic Exhibition in Dublin that summer. The Exhibition opened on 15 July 1914 with a lavish ceremony. In spite of the turbulent political and social backdrop of the summer of 1914, or perhaps because of that, the exhibition proved popular with the people of Dublin from the start.

Patrick Geddes, of course, presided over the Summer School of Civics. The Aberdeens provided hospitality and he dined regularly with the 'great and the good' of Ireland. One evening after dinner he was vigorously declaiming:

> I urge not only that the collections in the Linen Hall be preserved permanently, but that the re-planning scheme which wins the Viceroy's prize can be carried out courageously and beginning this very summer.

Later that same evening, Lord Aberdeen, having received a message, broke the news that war had started. It was 4 August 1914.

The next day Geddes wrote a most remarkably perceptive letter to Alasdair on the headed notepaper of the *Civic Exhibition*, Ireland, 1914, starting:

> As to the war, this is the fruition of past ideas and ideals and their applications: and it must now run its course; as such things do.

Obviously typed by Geddes in haste, full as it is of mistakes and misspellings, he sees that the pieces are properly placed on the board (a) for a first game of 'imperial destruction, international war and patriotic unities'. For the second game (b) 'the exasperated and angry people of every capital' will seek 'to do away with their incompetent rulers'. 'It is 1870–71 over again on a greater scale'. We must admire Geddes's foresight.

While thousands flocked to the colours for a show that would be over by Christmas, he foresaw the collapse of the Austrian, German, Ottoman and Russian Empires, revolution in Russia, mutiny and civil unrest in Germany and Austria, 'perhaps even in minor cities like this'. (The Easter Rising in Dublin began on Easter Monday, 24 April 1916).

Geddes raged against the:

> Gadarene rout of dying ideas and ideals, the legions of devils of the past entering into the people and driving them to ruin. Here are the devils of Machiavelli and the theorists and warriors of the balance of power, the old religious hatreds re-awakening, the old tyrannies and revolts. Here are the mechanical and the romantic ideas of the politicians, the jingo-isms of the imperialists and their bureaucracies, the protests of the Social-ists, the great doings of the financiers and the anarchic discontent they especially create.

He tells Alasdair that their duty is 'to work at and for better ideals and beginnings'.

> Just as in the war a trained officer is more valuable than a private and a staff officer more than a line one, so you and I have to keep back from the front and attend to our more difficult and important duties far in the rear of the immediate war of the better order which may be brought more nearly in and sooner than at present seems!

As we shall see, Geddes stuck to this view, while Alasdair, like the good lad he was, went along with his father until, tormented by indecision as to where his greater duty lay, he came back to volunteer for service.

In April 1914, Geddes had contracted to take his *Cities Exhibition* to the Madras Presidency in India, with him as planning consultant and Alasdair as assistant. In August, the Linen Hall in Dublin, his exhibition centre and headquarters of his planning activities in the city, was first turned into a barracks, then a training centre for nurses, then a hospital. On 6 September, Geddes and Alastair sailed for India on the P&O liner *Nore*. The Cities Exhibition was packed up and despatched separately in the *Clan Grant* – to complete catastrophe near the southern tip of India.

The cruise of the *Emden* was like a tale out of the *Boys' Own Paper*, showing a completely opposite side of the German character from the goings-on at Louvain. Germany had an overseas empire in Africa and around the Pacific. On 14 August, the German East Asia Squadron set off for Germany to defeat a British squadron at Cape Coronel off the coast of Chile, only to be destroyed in turn at the Falklands; while Captain von

Müller took the light cruiser *Emden* into the Indian Ocean, followed by four colliers so that he need not put in at any port for refuelling. With wireless telegraphy still at an early stage there now began a gigantic game of Blind Man's Buff in the vast spaces of the Indian Ocean. There would suddenly appear over the horizon this four-funnelled cruiser (von Müller had added a dummy funnel to make his ship look like the HMS *Yarmouth*) which would fire a shot across your bows, hoist the German ensign and signal: 'Stop at once. Do not wireless'. The crew and passengers would be taken off and the ship sunk. Neutral vessels would be released and given some of von Müller's 'guests' to take back to port.

Over 20 British ships were sunk by the *Emden*. On 16 October three British ships were sunk, including *Clan Grant* of 3,948 tons, with Geddes's precious exhibition aboard. On the night of 22 September *Emden* shelled the oil tanks of Madras (Chennai)[1] and on 28 October sailed at full speed into Penang harbour, sinking the *Zhemchug* (a Russian cruiser which had been sent to find and destroy *Emden*). The captain of the *Zhemchug* had been ashore seeing his mistress during the attack; he was subsequently demoted and imprisoned. A party of 60 Chinese prostitutes were aboard at the time of the action; their fate is unknown. *Emden* was pursued by a French destroyer, *Mousquet*, which was itself destroyed. The 36 survivors were picked up and transferred to a British steamer, which was then allowed to take them to Sumatra in the neutral Dutch East Indies.

Panic reigned around the Indian Ocean. Insurance rates shot up. It was a source of much embarrassment to the British and other Allies that a single German cruiser could effectively shut down the entire Indian Ocean.

Looking for *Emden*, the tiny needle in a vast haystack, were four vessels of the Imperial Japanese Navy, three French, two Russian and the British *Hampshire* and *Yarmouth*, HMS *Weymouth*, RMS *Empress of Russia* and SS *Empress of Australia*. Von Müller took his ship to the Cocos Islands in order to destroy the Eastern Telegraph Company wireless station. Fifty armed seamen went ashore and knocked down the radio tower (showing consideration for the tennis court!) – but not before a general call went out.

A mere 55 miles away the Australian light cruiser HMAS *Sydney* was escorting a convoy. Within three hours she had engaged the *Emden*, who had had to leave the boarding party on shore. Outgunned as she was, the battle lasted three hours till *Emden* was beached to avoid sinking. After further bombardment she surrendered having lost 131 dead and 65 wounded.[2]

The Cities Exhibition was a main source of Geddes's income, as well as his main visual aid. A lesser man would have crumbled but, as he wrote to Lord and Lady Aberdeen:

> The best I can say is that having raged so much over Louvain and other cities, I have not lost sleep over the loss of even the best of plans and pictures of them. Still it is hard... to lose years of work!

Back in Britain, Arthur and friends rallied round to stitch together a replacement Cities and Town Planning Exhibition which was shipped out to India in time to open in Madras on 17 January 1915, after Alasdair had worked frantically on its display.

In January 1915 Geddes requested leave of absence from his summer duties at Dundee, so that he might organise visits to those parts of Belgium 'as may be free from the Invader' in order to plan the reconstruction of the war-damaged towns. Ever the optimist!

In July he set up, supported by Anna, and led with a daily lecture, a

THE GERMAN SEA-RAIDER RUN TO GROUND

W. Burgess

S.M.S. (the German form of H.M.S.) *EMDEN* was a fast cruiser attached to the German Pacific fleet. In various disguises, she harried allied shipping, and even her foes could scarce forbear to cheer the colossal impudence and daring of some of her exploits when she disguised herself as a Japanese, French, or British craft. After a stern chase, however, H.M.A.S. *Sydney* caugh her off Keeling, Cocos Island and sank her on Novembe: 10. A wave of relief passed over all ship-owners a *Emden's* final demise.

Fig 1 The German sea raider run to ground (*Pageant of the Century*)

three-week Summer Meeting in King's College, London on 'The War: Its Social Tasks and Problems'. Over 40 professors, statesmen, MPs and relief workers, Serbians, Russians, Belgians and Dutch attended as well as members of such organisations as the National Home and Land League, the War Victims Relief Committee of the Society of Friends, the Professional Classes War Relief Council and the Royal Geographical Society.

Of interest were the apologies for absence. 'Military duties' prevented Charles Bathurst from attending:

> Percy Lovell cannot attend the summer course as he has enlisted in the Artists' Rifles and now has a commission with the Northumberland Fusiliers.

Arthur Percival Newton was unable to assist as he felt he had 'nothing to say about matters of material reconstruction after the war' as his work lay 'entirely on the political side'. From the Dublin School of Commerce, GJT Clampett wrote that it was unlikely that anyone would attend from Dublin 'as they are all giving up their vac to War Work'.

Sara Mackenzie-Kennedy (of Bournville) was one satisfied participant. She was so impressed by Geddes that she wrote to him for help in appointing a tutor who would convince her son that anti-militarist views were of greater worth than militarism.

Much of the rest of the war Geddes spent in India, where he learned of Alasdair's death, and Anna died. He retired from Dundee in 1919 and then accepted the Chair of Civics and Sociology in the University of Bombay (Mumbai). Somehow he managed to fit in the Reconstruction Front in France and Belgium.

From 1917 to 1925 he was involved in a project on *The Making of the Future*, involving three books and more than a score of pamphlets. He set out five 'sound stones' for building the 'Perfect City of the Future'. These were:

- To crush utterly the Prussian military machine and free the world, *including the German people*, from its menace for all time.
- To liberate the Allied peoples not only from the threat of Berlin *but from their own war-capitals as well; from the bureaucratic and financial octopuses* of Paris and London, Rome, New York and Washington.
- To rebuild both the war-torn areas of Belgium and France and *the*

industry-devastated slums of Liverpool, Chicago, and a hundred other cities behind the lines.

- To free schools and universities everywhere from their evil burden of lifelessness, *Germanic over-specialisms and repressive systems of 'cram and examine'.*
- To create a workable League of Nations guided and implemented by a Federation of Cities and a 'Concert of Universities'.

These were really quite stunning recommendations, which went far beyond the redrawing of international boundaries. With a rather touching naivety, Geddes and his colleagues believed that they had only to point out the real causes of world conflict, and to sketch the kind of material and spiritual reconstruction that people surely must be ready for by this time.

But in the real world of hard-nosed negotiation, who would even have bothered to read the words of an ivory-tower idealist in his late 60s? Clemenceau ('The Tiger') dominated the Peace Conferences. Germany must be made to pay for the full cost of the war, to hand back Alsace and Lorraine to France, to be stripped of her colonies and suffer other humiliations. And, as we know, the vengeful tactics of the victorious Allies helped to create the conditions from which Adolf Hitler emerged – and the League of Nations of competing nation-states collapsed in 1936.[3]

The story of Geddes the Peace Warrior is really not only a True Story, but a Sad Story, the story of one who was totally at odds with the spirit of the times, who knew he was right, but had too little power or influence to do more than engage a few like himself.

But with Geddes one must expect the unexpected. The Royal Navy was the ultimate guarantor for all British ships and cargoes. Each vessel lost to the enemy generated a payment to the ship's owner, while cargoes insured with private insurers were covered with a government insurance scheme. In 1926 the governmental war damage agency awarded Geddes £2,054 as compensation for the loss of the Cities Exhibition.

As Boardman says:

The kindly disposed reader will immediately wonder into which of his deficit undertakings this money was placed: the struggling Tower in Edinburgh, the cataloguing of its precious contents, or the repayment of overdrafts; or perhaps another college to be founded on more acres of dry heath, with the blasting out of more rocks to create more deficit vegetable gardens. But PG did none of these things with this windfall.

In fact his *Collége des Ecossais* came pretty close to this last option. What a marvellous man, that he should plunge into another imaginative scheme at an age when others would contemplate afternoons on the bowling green or gently poking the fire.

Anna Morton (1857–1917)

Anna Morton was the daughter of a successful Ulster Scots linen merchant in Liverpool. She was 'a highly educated young lady of great intelligence, not beautiful, but with great personal charm'. After a year in Dresden she could have, had she needed to, supported herself as a music teacher. She had a social conscience, set up a girls' club, was in contact with Octavia Hill and was involved in the incipient movement for the emancipation of women.

Anna's younger sister, Edith, had married a James Oliphant, headmaster of the Charlotte Square (Edinburgh) Institution for the Education of Girls and a friend of Geddes. The Oliphants held 'Secular Positivist' debating group meetings on social problems. Geddes, Oliphant and the Morton sisters were founder members of the 'Environmental Society' in 1884. A correspondence developed in 1885 until, on a Sunday early in 1886, Geddes proposed to Anna in the Royal Botanic Garden.

Six months after they were married they moved to James Court, a near-slum off the Lawnmarket in the Old Town of Edinburgh. This was the first of many moves, almost beyond the wit of man to chart, which bedevilled the life of poor Anna.

In James Court the Geddeses set about transforming the local community – cleaning up, painting and decorating, planting flowers, giving lessons on childcare and other good works. Patrick, of course, was away for substantial periods and once wrote, on returning:

> It is good to renew sympathy with one's fellows in their poverty once more; we have been too long away from the Lawnmarket and tend to forget; at least I do.

For Anna, however, there were few opportunities for escape from the demoralising grind of living amongst the poor.

After five years the first part of Geddes's superb development of Ramsay Garden was finished and a fine flat was available for the growing family there (with '15 rooms and two balconies'). But the family could not afford to keep it up, so it was always rented out to a senior officer from the adjacent Castle. The Geddes family only lived there in August during the Summer Meetings, when the Outlook Tower was the administrative centre and the Geddes flat the social centre, and Anna's music came into its own. In the summer term, Geddes was committed to Dundee and a house across the Tay at Newport was usually taken.

Anna Morton shared many of Geddes's ventures and some of his enthusiasms. Through his long absences and frequent changes of residence she kept the family together and its father on course. Geddes wrote persuasively about the importance of home education. Anna provided and organised it. Geddes was frequently on the edge of bankruptcy and Anna was the rock on which he was able to build his creative life. Anna had 'her full share of moral earnestness', and:

> Both were moved by the new spirit of social service and both had a streak of puritan severity in their idealism. Their rejection of the religious ideas of their parents did not incline them to laxity in self-discipline; it made them rather less tolerant of self-indulgence, sometimes in others as well as in themselves.

Arthur Geddes, 40 years after his mother's death, wrote:

> Patrick and Anna, man and wife, achieved and maintained success through all their adventures together and apart. Without Anna, without the intimate relationship they made together, Patrick's flashes of discovery might have lacked the fire which sustained thought and civic action. Without her he could not have dwelt so continuously nor with such understanding in the sick core of the Old Town. A great-hearted man with many faults, he could not have attained his moral stature without her ardour of love, faith, and clear-eyed critique. She too felt herself fortunate, in spite of the difficulties of sharing so nomadic a life, so many anxieties and risks. Anxious friends frequently condemned the risks; but the decisions were shared. And Anna, as musician, kept ready to resume teaching if need be, as her valued friend Marjory Kennedy-Fraser had done when left a widow. She knew that, should the worst befall, she could face the future. Her children knew only that she played and sang for her own sake and theirs and because she loved it.

Amelia Defries, while Geddes was still alive, wrote of the 'Exposition Internationale' at Ghent in 1913. PG arrived late, but fortunately:

His wife came with him, the calm grey-haired lady who could bring order out of chaos. Even more valuable… was her power of intercession, her ability to tone down Pat's cerebral high-voltage when some bewildered soul was in danger of electrocution.

As Miss Defries said:

Mrs Geddes found time, while sorting books and jotting down notes, to enquire as to my health and living arrangements; and a few days later she had me in much better rooms, working shorter hours and living more normally than during the last three months.

Clearly this was a marriage of true minds and they continued to write each other love letters for all of their married lives. Yet there is a suggestion that they were so close and so busy that the efficient organisation of the children left little space for 'over-flowing mother-love', as Arthur phrased it, or, as Paddy Kitchen suggests, the constant need for discipline quelled spontaneity and the expression of personal instincts.

Even Alasdair, loyal, courageous, trustworthy Alasdair, could say: 'no human being could live as well as work with PG and survive'. Yet Anna survived for over 30 years of marriage and, at the end, Geddes felt he had to use subterfuge to conceal Alasdair's death from her, to spare her one last blow.

At the outbreak of war Anna was 57 years old, with a complex web of commitments and responsibilities she had to handle on her own – plus two sons, Alasdair (23) and Arthur (19), of a very suitable age for going to war.

For the first winter of the war her husband and Alasdair were in India. In 1915 she was heavily involved in the three-week Summer Meeting in King's College, London on 'The War: Its Social Tasks and Problems'. While this was Geddes's triumph much of the organisation and half the guest list were Anna's.

Much of 1915 was spent in networking – in a letter to Arthur she wrote:

There must be justice before there can be real or permanent peace. Many things have to be considered, therefore; but we were all united in agreeing that it is women's work in particular to promote peace, and that there are many ways of influencing the public mind towards peace, just as there are endless opportunities for the reverse. We bound ourselves not to interfere with the conduct of the present war.

In 1916, Geddes contributed to an *Exposition de la Ville Reconstituée* in Paris. Geddes was in Dundee, fulfilling his teaching obligations, and Anna was left in Paris to struggle with the exhibits and to organise 'distant and uncertain lecturers by correspondence.' Very loyally she remonstrated with her husband about putting too much into his programme. Mildly she wrote on 10 June – the day before the opening – that she 'was supposed to cover the 180 sq metres in the one day!' Two days later she wrote:

> I don't see how I am to prepare any programme with so little to go up as you give me – No fixed dates; save that you arrive sometime before 9 July... No word either from or of Mr Fleure.[4]

Late in 1916, Geddes returned to India, accompanied by Anna. For the first half of 1917 things went very well for him, with plenty of work and receptive audiences – 'a very distinct phase of intensified lucidity & vision'. Anna, however, had dysentery and fever and Geddes wrote to Alasdair of the need for her protection from anxiety. Anna should have been sent back to Britain to avoid the hot weather but this was impossible because sea passages to Britain for women and children were refused because of the U-boat menace.

So the couple began to plan for a Summer Meeting in Darjeeling. But in April, Geddes received a cable informing him of Alasdair's death in action. Fearful of the effect of this news on Anna's health, Geddes did not inform Anna. As Alasdair's weekly letters continued to arrive by mail steamer, Geddes would read them out to his ailing wife.

From the hospital in Lucknow, Geddes took Anna to stay just outside Calcutta with an Indian doctor known to them from his student days in Edinburgh. (The first Indian graduated from the University of Edinburgh in 1876.) Anna was far from well – it is suggested that she was carrying enteric (typhoid) fever contracted in the hospital in Lucknow. Geddes was in a dilemma but Anna insisted that he carry out his Darjeeling commitment.

Partly thanks to Anna's organisation the Darjeeling meeting was a great success. Geddes was kept furiously busy, although he found time for a daily letter to Anna.

He planned to visit her the first weekend in June. But the doctors discouraged the trip at this time for fear the news of Alasdair's death might have to be told, since his letters had ceased arriving. A week later a wire summoned Geddes to Calcutta in all haste. The journey took 22 hours, and in the meantime Anna succumbed to the fever despite all efforts to prolong her life.

Poor Anna! A Sad Story, even sadder because of its truth. Even at the end unwilling to hold back her mercurial husband. Dying alone in a land so far and so different from her several homes. And yet, at the end, there was a liberal comradeship. Some weeks later, Geddes wrote to Amelia Defries:

> I spent the day beside her – and then in evening the old Indian students she had mothered, as they said, when in Edinburgh... came at short notice, all in Indian costume and barefoot and carried her, six by six, on an open funeral bier all the three miles to the Crematorium, I following... Then on the steps all sang Rabindranath Tagore's 'Farewell' – a strangely penetrating funeral hymn, and they sprinkled incense over her and flowers... and so now have but her ashes to bring home.

Norah Geddes (1887–1967)

In old age Lady Mears wrote a memoir of 200 pages, describing her early life. Although it peters out about 1910, it still offers a glimpse of the feelings of a Geddes child towards war.

The Geddes flat in Ramsay Garden, with its two balconies, has a splendid view over the Castle Esplanade and up to the Castle. While the Geddeses could only afford to use the flat during the Summer Meetings, Norah enjoyed the view when young, when:

> There was always a battalion of a Scots regiment quartered in the castle in those days and the spectacle of their parade drill made a great impression on me, it was a factor in my life. Their precision of movement had an influence on me.

She remembered the departure of the Black Watch for the Boer War with Andy Wauchope on a black charger (with his high bridged nose and his red hair).

The Highland Soldier as wished for – and in action – is seen in the South African War Black Watch memorial on The Mound, just below Edinburgh Castle. PLATES 1A and 1B. Less romantic are the lists on the base.

> Killed in Action or Died of Wounds – 14 Officers and 121 Other Ranks.
>
> Died from Disease – One Officer and 76 Other Ranks.

Surely an indictment of the British Army's support services.

So much for the pageantry of war; the uniforms, the drill, the pipes. And then:

> I recall the impression of distress made on my father by the battle of Magersfontein: the Black Watch regiment was decimated in the autumn of '99 and he was glad his father had been spared the news because that was his old regiment.[5]

Norah grew up under the Geddes 'home education' system and benefited from it in that she had many enriching experiences and, in particular, developed an interest in and love of growing things. She determined to become a garden designer and landscape architect – but there was no specialized course available to her. So, in effect, she joined the family business and worked on Geddes's and the Edinburgh Social Union's gardens in Edinburgh. Geddes designed the Edinburgh Zoo and Norah was responsible for sections of that. From 1911 to 1914 she was in Dublin, creating gardens in the corners of the slums as the follow-up to the Cities and Town Planning Exhibition and the subsequent national health policy, development plan and programme of activities.

Geddes, of course, was an idealist and his view of the beauty of physical labour was not always appreciated by lesser mortals. Thus Norah wrote on 19 October 1910:

> This afternoon Miss Le Maistre and I and two helpers were working in the Open Spaces. While I was alone in the King Wall, hordes of boys came in and made a regular bear garden, watering the soaking ground, tying the hose in knots, scraping up the ash, threatening each other with the dangerous ends of the hoes, and swinging on the posts. They declared at intervals that they were all on strike. I took it more or less as a joke and got them off in a little while to the West Port carrying some tools. Of course the problem is a difficult one. Where enough to give so many to do in a small garden?

And again on 30 November:

> I am very tired of grubbing in the Open Spaces and count on this week being the last – one thousand small bulbs, at 50 for 1/-, have just been landed on us and I wonder how many of the miserable things will flower... Mr. Mears seems very active just now and sends me strange diagrams, and discourses on art and symbolism.

Mr Mears was, of course, Frank Mears, Secretary of the Open Spaces Committee, Geddes's second-in-command and collaborator in, for example, the Photographic Survey of Edinburgh of 1905, for which he drew an excellent series of sketches showing the growth of Edinburgh. Mears went on to have 'a good war'. As Captain Mears he served under Alasdair (Major Geddes) in the Royal Flying Corps as a forward observation officer for the artillery. After the war he ceased to work in Geddes's shadow and went into practice on his own.

On the Home Front, World War 1 saw a shortage of labour on farms and in gardens as the men went off to war. Lady gardeners were in demand for servicing the heating systems of greenhouses on the big estates as well as planting and cultivation and Norah busied herself in related organisations at home and in Belgium – the Geddes connection again. For example, in October 1916 Amy McGregor wrote to Norah asking her to find a lady gardener to plan a garden at the new house on Loch Striven of her sister, Lady Anderson.

Norah and Mears were married in 1916 and Norah's life became that of the conventional wife and mother, her three sons Kenneth, Alasdair and John being born, respectively, in 1917, 1918 and 1921. Geddes tried to tie her in to the family by making over to her the furnishings and contents of 14 Ramsay Garden. These had belonged to Anna but the flat had had to be sold to the Town and Gown Association. Nevertheless the Mears family continued to live at 14 Ramsay Garden and Norah, in effect, managed the Outlook Tower. In 1931 she set up an 'Outlook Tower class' for pupils of low attainment in conventional education. Run on Geddesian lines it attracted a clientele for whom – for example – special arrangements were made with the Central Library.

Norah's story began with her looking over the Castle Esplanade to the Castle, with its romantic silhouette and history. In the 1920s, the old North Barracks of 1755 were rebuilt to become the Scottish National War Memorial. In 1944, the Moray Press in Edinburgh published *Intimations and Awards,* a collection of poems by Norah G Mears. Her poem about the Scottish National War Memorial in effect closes the circle of the view from the Geddes flat in Ramsay Garden.

The Edinburgh Castle War Memorial

Grey looms the castle's battlemented line,
Enclosing memory's jewelled shrine.
Its pilgrims climb the cobbled street,
Some sore at heart, and dragging weary feet.

Were they but here to see these same grey walls
When dawn's red glow upon them falls;
Whose mass all lapis-lazuli,
Is set against a lucent turquoise sky.

By mist invested, see the turrets proud
Rise from the haar's beleaguering cloud:
Or silhouetted 'gainst the flare
By night, in thunderstorm's fierce blare.

From sorrow, weary souls can find reprieve
In loveliness that changes morn and eve:
Can shed some clinging weight of grief or age
And find the peace that's won by pilgrimage.

And so it was in the memorial shrine;
Carved stone, stained glass, rich bronze of rare design
Show deeds wherein their valiant sons took part,
When God caught up and gathered to His heart.

Alasdair Geddes (1891–1917)

Survey, an important American Periodical of the time, in 1925, ran a series of six *Talks from My Outlook Tower* by Patrick Geddes. In *The Education of Two Boys* he vigorously attacked the 'cram-exam' system and boarding schools and put forward a most persuasive case for home education.

Alasdair Geddes was one of the two boys in Geddes's essay, the other being Geddes himself. Alasdair had an education of Head, Heart and Hand, a home education broadened by travel and changes of residence and by 'work experience' – as a mason, as a shepherd, on an experimental farm, and in the Millport Zoological Station. He qualified as a lifeboat steersman, broke horses for army use and, at 18, served on Bruce's Arctic exploration of 1909. (Mount Geddes and Alasdair Horn commemorate his survey work.)

Feeling the need to qualify formally for university entrance he had a year at Edinburgh Academy where, after a slow start, he became dux of his class. He is also likely to have served in the OTC (Officers' Training Corps) – he was a piper – and obtained the necessary minimal qualification for a commission in the Army. Somehow 'he graduated BSC with the highest honours'.

In 1914, Alasdair was 23 years old. He was gentle and sensitive in character, but cheerful. Above all, he was practical and totally reliable, doing the donkey work on his father's projects. He and Anna were Geddes's main supports and moderators of the great man's worst excesses. Geddes, on the other hand, may have been honest but was certainly unpleasant when he said of Alasdair, when aged nine: 'What a pity that courageous people will be so stupid'.

At the beginning of the war, Alasdair went as his father's assistant to India. Soon

> He was tormented by his dilemma as to where his duty lay: to his country and her war-ravaged allies, or to his father's work.

His mother, understandably, tried her best to dissuade her son from enlisting. His father also tried to keep him under his wing and return to India with him, his argument being that he could do more good helping to create a better post-war India than by getting lost in the huge killing machine in Western Europe.

Alasdair countered by turning his father's romantic teaching against him, saying:

> It is not for nothing that you have given me Highland blood and name; the clan feeling will not be merged in foreign empire when the clan is pressed. Now, the clan is France, is Europe: when these call, let the East wait.

Alasdair came through France on his way home from India and so must have picked up a little of what was going on there. Once home, he did not march enthusiastically into the nearest recruiting office. We are all familiar with the young First World War subaltern, fresh from his public school, going over the top with a distinctive uniform and pistol which marked him out for enemy snipers. 'Stupid' Alasdair clearly knew what he was doing – probably with his cousin as a model – and with care and thoroughness set about inquiries and investigations as to how and where he could render the most effective service.

First, he learned how to drive heavy motor vehicles, then learned to fly at Roehampton School of Aeronautics before being commissioned into the Royal Naval Air Service. For once, the military recognised that here was a square peg ideally suited for fitting into a square hole and he was transferred into the 17th Kite Balloon Company of the Royal Flying Corps. (The RNAS was amalgamated with the RFC to form the RAF on 1 April 1918, and by the end of the war over 3,000 personnel were engaged in aerial photo interpretation.)

The Duke of Wellington attributed success in warfare to knowing what was going on 'on the other side of the hill'. The big guns can easily fire on targets on the other side of the hills – at one point in the Great War, shells were being fired into central Paris from 60 miles away – but how can the gunners be sure where to aim, or whether the target has been hit?

In March 1918 a 'supergun' opened fire on Paris from a distance of 70 miles. Aimed at the Louvre, not one shot hit this huge target – but every miss did damage in the city. On Good Friday, the Church of St Gervais was struck during Mass. Seventy-five were killed outright, 90 were injured and many more died later. One wonders by how long this action short-ened the course of the war and whether it was remembered when the Peace Conferences were taking place.

In the Great War, the answer was to have a Forward Observation Officer close to the target to report back on the accuracy – or otherwise – of the battery's fire. Or he could go up high – to the top of a church tower, or up in a balloon, or in a spotter plane – for general reconnais-sance, or for spotting the fall of shot on enemy positions.

Ian Hay's, *The First Hundred Thousand*, gives us a good illustration of the Forward Observation Officer at work, worth quoting extensively:

One afternoon the Highlanders come under heavy artillery fire.

Then comes a pause. A message is passed down for stretcher-bearers. Things are growing serious.

Captain Blaikie looks grave.

'Better ring up the Gunners, I think. Where are the shells coming from?'

That wood on our left front, I think.'

'That's P27. Telephone orderly, there?'

A figure appears in the doorway.

'Yes, sir.'

'Ring up Major Cavanagh, and say that H21 is being shelled from P27. Retaliate!'

'Verra good, sir.'

The telephone orderly disappears, to return in five minutes.

'Major Cavanagh's compliments, sir, and he is coming up himself for tae observe from the firing trench.'

'Good egg!' observes Captain Blaikie. 'Now we shall see some shooting, Bobby.'

Presently the Gunner major arrives, accompanied by an orderly, who pays out wire as he goes.

'Number one gun!' chants the major, peering into his periscope; 'three-five-one-nothing – lyddite – fourth charge!'

The major stiffens to his periscope, and Bobby Little, deeply interested, wonders what has become of the report of the gun. He forgets that sound does not travel much faster than a thousand feet a second and that the guns are a mile and a half back. Presently, however, there is a distant boom. Almost simultaneously the lyddite shell passes overhead with a scream. Bobby, having no periscope, cannot see the actual result of the shot, though he tempts Providence by peering over the top of the parapet.

After some adjustment the major commands crisply:

'Parallel lines on number one. One round battery fire – twenty seconds!'

For the last time the order is passed down the wire, and the major hands the periscope to the ever-grateful Bobby, who has hardly got his eyes to the glass when the round of battery fire commences. One – two – three – four – the avenging shells go shrieking on their way, at intervals of twenty seconds. There are four muffled thuds, and four great columns of earth and debris soaring up before the wood. Answer comes there none. The offending battery has prudently effaced itself.

'Cease fire!' says the major, 'and register!' Then he turns to Captain Blaikie.

'That'll settle them for a bit,' he observes.

Alasdair had a good war. His unconventional education fitted him very well for the more complex side of warfare, and his first Commanding Officer said he had 'a genius for observation'. He was good at 'spotting'.

As Alasdair wrote to his sister Norah:

> We've had another two or three really good days or half-days. Last time
> we registered 'direct hits' on two different houses which we were ranging
> for two different batteries. It is very exhilarating after straining to see
> whether the little puffs of grey-black smoke are over or short, to see the
> target go up in huge clouds of smoke and red brick-dust...

An observer in a kite-balloon was a great danger to the enemy and
therefore an obvious target – and
an easy one – for his gunners and
snipers, and Alasdair had a few
lucky escapes.

Siegfried Sassoon had another
slant on the balloon officer:

> Young Holt... had escaped from
> the Infantry into the Balloon
> Section. He felt that RFC officers
> had a social superiority to the
> Infantry. Being up in a balloon
> elevated a man in more ways
> than one, and he often aired his
> discrimination in such matters.

Fig 2 A German Forward Observation Officer
bails out of his burning balloon
Pageant of the Century

Let Ian Hay take over. Captain
Wagstaffe and Bobby Little are discussing the role of the artillery.
Bobby thought that loosing off the
big guns must be great sport.

'They tell me it's a greatly overrated amusement,' replied Wagstaffe, 'like
posting an insulting letter to someone you dislike. You see, you aren't
there when he opens it at breakfast next morning! The only man of them
who gets any fun is the Forward Observing Officer. And he,' concluded
Wagstaffe in an unusual vein of pessimism, 'does not live long enough to
enjoy it!'

Alasdair's unit was stationed at the south end of the British lines, next to
the French and Alasdair was particularly useful – with the good French
all the family spoke – in liaison with them. On the ground he acted as a

field instructor for other observers and adapted some of the best French practice.

Off duty, he busied himself with occupying the men's time usefully. He had them gardening and, borrowing the horses used to drag the guns, taught them the skill of ploughing.

He was promoted to Captain and then, in December 1916, at the age of 25, to Major. It may be that he was the youngest Major in – what? ¬ The army? Unlikely. The RFC? Perhaps. He was awarded the Military Cross for 'an act or acts of exemplary gallantry during active operations against the enemy' and the Cross of the Légion d'Honneur for his liaison work with the French.

Geddes aficionados may have noticed slight differences between the above and the printed accounts of Alasdair's war service. Clearly Alasdair's promotion was swift and well-deserved. What is not mentioned by the likes of Mairet and – very strangely – by his Commanding Officer two months after his death, is that his Service Record shows that, when he was killed, he was Acting Lieutenant-Colonel. More proof of his value, if it were needed.

As the letter to Norah implies, gunners are usually spared from close observation of the results of their labours – as the 'Poor Bloody Infantry' are not. But they are subjected to retaliatory fire from the enemy guns. Alasdair was killed on 19 April 1917. One account of his death goes like this:

> One day he was walking back to his unit from an observation post in front of the artillery lines and was struck by a shell fragment. He was killed instantly.

Another, slightly different, says that he and two other officers were making their way back to the lines when the enemy opened fire. The three officers took refuge in a shell-hole only big enough for two. Alasdair volunteered to 'find a better 'ole' but was killed on his way to it.[6]

Writing to 'Dear Professor Geddes' on 29 June 1917 from 'In the Field', Alasdair's Commanding Officer said:

> Your son from the very first took everything seriously and it was easy for me to see that he was sure to make a name for himself as an observer. There is no doubt that his training with you before the war enabled him to become so proficient in so short a time. Map reading and accurately placing on the map what is seen from the air is our chief work and you

will understand that came readily to him with his knowledge of maps. His devotion to duty and care of his officers and men made me put his name forward for promotion at an early date. He was invaluable to me and I miss him everyday, as we did so many things together. I was simply devoted to him and I hope and think he liked me both as a friend and his commanding officer. Although he quickly rose to being made a Major, I am certain there was no one who but said he richly deserved it, he was loved by all his men and officers, but at the same time there was no lack of discipline among them. I fear I may not write about the work he did (because of censorship) but sincerely hope I may one day be able to tell you in full of all his doings, how he was rewarded with the MC etc. I was proud to see he has also been awarded a French decoration which he would have been so pleased and honoured to have got.

Did I tell you that we buried him very simply as I knew he would have liked? Mears, another officer and myself, were present, a Scotch Clergyman read a very nice service and then as if they knew, the guns, that he had ranged so well, boomed out on all sides, as if to pay him a last tribute. The dear boy lies there now, and the guns are all about him, until we move forward again.

Patrick received the news in India by cable. Anna was far from well and Patrick felt unable to break the bad news to her. Alasdair's weekly letters continued to arrive by mail steamer. Patrick would read them aloud to Anna. Perhaps fortunately, Anna died without having learned of her son's death.

The double blow of 1917 was devastating for Geddes. Although he bounced back to have another 15 very active years, he never really recovered the impetus and self-confidence his two main helpmeets had given him.

As a result of an education of 'Head, Heart and Hand', Arthur Geddes had become a proficient woodcarver. In 1918 Patrick suggested to his son that he carve a memorial shrine to his brother. On 6 November – five days before the Armistice – Arthur wrote to his father, having made a few sketches, saying that he would do something with his guidance:

It's sad to do it, yet I feel that the balance lies the other way for me and that it is a relief to turn sorrow to expression of love and reverence. If one can do it expression helps in the transmutation of leaden grief to something finer, something winged.

Clearly Arthur was successful in his enterprise. The beautifully tranquil result shows Saint Theodore – senior to Saint George in the Greek Orthodox countries – transfixing the evil dragon.

Good triumphs over evil. If only it were true. Alasdair's story was True but Sad, the saddest thing about it being the fact that the Peace Warrior's liberal and practical education had perfectly trained his son for one of the most dangerous roles in modern warfare, setting him up for an almost certain death.

In 1921 Geddes visited Alasdair's grave. He wrote to Norah:

> As you know, it was at first alone, but 30 or 40 more now surround it, in a little enclosure. The cross stands all right; the inscription from his comrades, though weathered, is still readable; and the box plant growing too.

SAINT THEODORE
IN MEMORY OF
ALASDAIR GEDDES, 1891–1917.
CARVED for A WEST HIGHLAND SHRINE
BY A.G. ca 1919.

Fig 3
Arthur's Memorial Shrine to his brother.
Marion Geddes

> Need I tell you how I sobbed over it; as the day of news from years ago. Hardy too could not but join me; and our good chauffeur broke down too when we came back to the road, and saw our faces, and he too had had his sorrows. (Do not think me so absorbed as to have lost feeling, or for any of you all!)

Arthur Geddes (1895–1968)

Every Scottish schoolboy knows that the Schlieffen Plan should have worked – and almost did. The German armies smashed their way through Belgium and across northern France and it looked certain that France would be knocked out of the war in six weeks. But on 27 August the plan was modified. The drive to the English Channel was left on hold and 'von Kluck's turn' took his First Army to within 30 miles of Paris, where it ground to a halt, exhausted.

And now took place what was later to be represented as a kind of military miracle – 'Joan of Arc won the Battle of the Marne'. While the French government fled to Bordeaux on 2 September, the French Fifth Army, after successive defeats and retreats, regrouped and recovered its French *élan*. Von Kluck later talked of 'the extraordinary and peculiar aptitude of the French soldier to recover quickly' which was 'a possibility not studied in our war academy'.

The British came in on the French left. In Paris, on 7 September, 600 taxis were assembled, each taking on board five poilus with their equipment, and made two trips to the front line – as General Gallieni, the Military Governor of Paris, said: 'Well, here at least is something out of the ordinary!'

More conventional reinforcements poured in. On 6 September the Allied counter-offensive began. The Battle of the Marne lasted till 12 September, by which date the Germans had been driven back 40 miles to beyond the Aisne, where they dug themselves in and remained for the rest of the war. Casualties on both sides totalled over 400,000.

The postcard which is shown as FIG 4 was sent by Arthur Geddes to his mother in Monifieith on 10 May 1915. It is interesting to note that

2. Bataille de la Marne (du 6 au 12 Septembre 1914) — GLANNES - Grande-Rue

Fig 4 Glannes, Grande Rue, 1915
Marion Geddes

commercial postcards of the recent battlefield were available so soon after the battle. Arthur's message is worth quoting in full:

> This is a village which is only ½ kilometer from Huiron, and which gives an idea of the ruin. In the distance X is one of our *barquements* a three-roomed 12 or 14m x 3 (or 4). Most of the chimneys are knocked down for safety. There are half a dozen houses at the far end of the village, at one of which we get our milk. The people there have had seven out of ten cattle burnt. They are very nice folk indeed. People are very short of fodder for their beasts which are mostly under-fed. In the winter many non-army horses had to live on *roseaux* (reeds), and got frightfully thin. They are not so bad now. The folk seem kind to their beasts here. Next time I shall send you my better card... with two fellows who worked here with me. Love, Arthur.

The question is: who was Arthur? And what was he doing in last year's battlefield?

Arthur was the youngest of the family; he came after Norah by eight years and Alasdair by four. His mother was 38 when he was born. He was said to be a 'brilliant and promising child – with nerves'. Norah and Alasdair were very close but, as the youngest, Arthur spent much of his time on his own, while home education and the semi- nomadic Geddes life militated against lasting friendships with children of his own age. Two successive winter terms in a Board School with classes of 60 did little for him. Arthur's imaginative and nervous temperament needed time to be understood and time was at a premium *chez* Geddes.

At the outbreak of war, Arthur Geddes was 19 and had just passed the University Prelim Exam. As he was not in good health he was sent to Barbreck in the West Highlands, where he did odd jobs on the farm of a family friend. On 27 September his father wrote to him about a placement he had arranged through a Mr Campbell. Patrick said that:

> I have told him that while we do not encourage you to join the army we *want* you to have the discipline and the hardship which are the good side of the military life. More than that of course we want you to feel that to work for peace, for a better life for your country, for your compatriots, needs as strenuous a preparation as for war, and that you need *more* determination, more self-control, more fitness, physical, intellectual and moral for this than for war... others will be thinking us failing in our duty to our country that we do not encourage you to at least join the territorials. You must not shame us by taking an easier life than your

comrades and acquaintances. Be as punctual and as strenuous as if you were under military discipline. Do not be afraid to let Mr Campbell know what you think you are capable of doing – help with his garden, clean his boots, peel potatoes – let him see that you can draw, that you can sing, play, dance, talk Gaelic... Think of all the things that might be useful to him and his people.

'His people' were the Friends' War Victims' Relief Committee, for whom Arthur was to spend most of the war working. In May 1915, we find him based on the *Mission Anglaise* in Huiron in the Marne. This was still in the War Zone in which 'precautions against espionage are greater and greater as they are nearer the front'.

> When the first 'FW Victims' came here they had an officer to look after them and inspect their work passports... twice a week. Now that the military know us we are very untroubled, and our uniforms go a long way of course. But the censorship of letters etc is still as strict of course.

His first posting had him in an *Equipe* of six, initially constructing their own quarters – a hut of weatherboarding, with one big room – seven by four metres – with a lean-to on the eastern gable for the kitchen, then the *barquements* for refugees. There was a lot of heavy work, shifting and carting bales and so forth. Besides his practical skills, Arthur had two other attributes which made him a valued member of any team. Like all the Geddeses, he was fluent in French, (he wrote home occasionally in French) which marked him out from his strongly Anglophone co-workers – and enhanced his value to the Mission. Also, he had the music, and could raise morale in a few moments.

One day he wandered off along a burn which flowed in beautiful curves through the chalk bordered by willows, just showing green, to find the bleached little wooden crosses of French graves. Usually they were nameless, but this plot was kept green by someone 'for an unknown countryman':

> The only sign of a German grave is that mound inside a half-filled shell-hole. Poor fellows how far from home they are! One sees the swift tragedy of it, the scattered fighting, advance and retreat extraordinarily vividly with these scattered graves, the ripped and felled trees and great shell-holes. Yet still the spring is breaking out in wonder of fresh green and blossom and wild flower.

In a foretaste of the future, Arthur found the work hard.

> This week I felt jolly tired every evening. We have had one of the hottest weeks they have had here for some years at this season… with thunder in the evening the last three days. We have also been trying a new way of working – getting up at 3.30am and working till 6.00am, then after breakfast, till 11.00am, lunch-time. We start again at 3.00pm when it is cooler and work till about 5.30pm, or as it has recently worked out, till about 6.30pm. Each of these four days on which we have tried this scheme I have had my midday sleep interrupted – by two local women, by a Breton soldier who wanted a meat safe made 'as the poor beggars have no such luxuries', and by two Scouts who had to be entertained.

From his next posting, Arthur wrote to his mother, describing his work:

> The work of the 'Maison' here is that of looking after some 60 'refugees' or *'repatriés'*; almost all women and children. It is not really a sanatorium as such but rather a preventive place, with perhaps one or two doubtful cases. In the case of refugees who generally come from Paris and the towns, there is generally something specific, whereas with the *repatriés* what is really needed is a little care and feeding, poor things. This means that the refugees generally stay longer (up to six months) while for the *repatriés* it is rather a jumping-off place, till they can join their people and get work somewhere (and they often stay about 1 month). Altogether this means that there's not much nursing on the part of the staff and a good deal of the work consists in looking after the children.

> My own job is fairly short and simple, about five hours a day & consists of 1) writing a certain number of letters per day, in French or English, re patients, accounts etc, all of which occupies one's mind and is quite good for me. 2) Keeping what accounts there are. 3) Looking after 10 or 12 boys if and when they are not at school (including bathing them twice a week which is quite a lark!)

> They are quite a nice little crowd, some of them with plenty of character and it is interesting to see what a variety of that there is. They are from six to 11 at the moment. If individualized, they are also fairly individualistic and without much sense of give and take or united effort such as our games give, I had never realized to what extent. We sometimes try games, but generally go walks, with racing and chasing on the way. There are one or two extremely interested in nature, apart from catching bugs or picking flowers!

Besides the looking after of these (every afternoon for about one and three-quarter hours) there are odd jobs which I generally manage in the afternoon or between 6.00pm and 7.30pm – Supper, B'fast at 8.00am, lunch 12.30pm.

By 1916, the cream of the British Army had been destroyed and The First Hundred Thousand were already going the same way. Volunteering was clearly not going to keep the war effort alive. So the Military Service Act was passed, specifying that single men aged 14 to 41 years old were liable to be called up for military service unless they were widowers with children or ministers of religion. Military Service Tribunals were set up to adjudicate on claims for exemption on the grounds of performing civilian work of national importance, domestic hardship, health, and conscientious objection.

Arthur must have received his call-up papers, whereupon a whirlwind of activity overtook the Geddes family. His mother made her position clear:

I feel this war is one of Governments and of particular interests, not of people's (tho' the peoples have been persuaded of its necessity). I think we women ought to realise that we may work towards peace by educating the future generations for peacedom instead of wardom, and by doing what in us lies towards bringing together the different classes whose economic interests clash, and getting them to understand each other's position.

And in another letter, Anna said that she felt that Arthur was 'doing as good work for France, dear, as Alasdair', who had now enlisted.

Alasdair wrote, pointing out the 'danger of our not winning' the war '*thoroughly* enough' (Alasdair's underlining), and repeating his reasons for joining up. Norah, who had just married Frank (Captain) Mears, wrote that she was surprised to find that Arthur was appealing on the score of 'conscientious objection'. It was hardly possible for her to be willing to have her husband join, and to think her younger brother should stand aside on conscientious grounds.

Conscientious objectors, of course, had a tough time, being exposed to public humiliation by patriotic women and harassment by the authorities. Siegfried Sassoon, who knew a thing or two about reluctance to fight, in *Memoirs of an Infantry Officer* writes:

I hadn't formed any opinion about Conscientious Objectors, but I couldn't help thinking that they must be braver men than some I'd seen wearing uniforms in safe places and taking salutes from genuine soldiers.

Anna wrote from Lucknow, suggesting that Arthur was:

Helping in the best way you can, that you could not be as useful as a Tommy as you are in your present capacity – that the Friends work needs support.

Perhaps feeling that Arthur was weakening as a result of Norah's letter, Anna wrote at greater length three weeks later.

I trust it may not be too late to confirm you in holding by the Friends – if confirmation you need. Though we do not hold the supernatural views of some of their members we are psychologically and socially Quakers, and you having joined them from conviction are one, and should stand beside them... You have no reason to feel 'side tracked' after the war seeing you have been working for more than a year now with a body affiliated to the French *Service de Santé Militaire*; and you have been accustomed to be independent of public opinion when that is opposed to your own convictions.

She brings in Patrick to reinforce the view that:

Not only are you better fitted for your present work than for the regular army, but that on that account you are more useful where you are, both for the present and the future. Do not fear therefore to call yourself a Quaker – you have a right to be a member of their community, both from your convictions and your work with them.

Charles Murray in *Dockens Afore his Peers* (*Exemption Tribunal*) described, with 'biting reality', one Exemption Tribunal, with John Watt of Dockenhill wriggling out of a tight corner:

There's men eneuch in sooter's shops, an' chiels in mason's yards'
An' counter-loupers, sklaters, vrichts an' quarrymen, an' cyuards,
To fill a reg'ment in a week, without gyaun vera far.
Jist shove them in ahin' the pipes, an' tell them that it's 'War'.

Murray's last line shows the relationship between Dockens and the Tribunal: – '"Total exemption'. Thank ye, sirs. Fat say ye till a dram?"

In April 1916, Arthur was with the Friends in Chambéry in the French Alps, where he learned from Norah (by telegraph) the result of his tribunal

– but no details. T Edmund Harvey MP told Patrick Geddes that he was 'glad that Arthur will not have to be persecuted for his beliefs', but Arthur was not excused military service on conscientious grounds, but because he was declared medically unfit.

Without going into tedious detail, Arthur's health came and went and, although his work was always valued and praised, it is clear that all was not well. It seems that, when on leave in Gloucestershire, he had written in to Headquarters suggesting that he go back to France as a part-time worker. In a very tactful reply, the Hon Secretary made it clear that 'we are not able to welcome you back while your health is not satisfactory'.

For the last few months of the war, Arthur was based near Lincoln at the Lincoln Stores District Park. He was now 3rd Clerk; he had a number – AG2832486 RAF – and a uniform. He worked in the Quartermaster's Stores, in the pay office, 'with zero to do', – a non-combatant role. He also had 'overtime in the evening unloading lorries, which made me a bit tired'. He attended parades, slept in a tent and took his turn on fire picquet. He was fairly fit and getting fitter – physically and mentally.

He had a full life after hours, playing his fiddle to the men in the canteen:

> They're very keen, a little disappointed at my ignorance of ragtime, but quite liking the Scots music – reels etc. and a few favourites like Loch Lomond. There are also opera airs, quite good… Next Sunday is a monthly church parade for Cathedral and the 'orchestra' accompanies one of the 2nd Lieutenants, a nice chap with an alto voice – 'Divine Redeemer', I think. On other Sundays… service in the canteen. The 'orchestra' plays for hymns. Then there was outreach – playing to convalescent wounded at a small VAD hospital.

Three letters to his father, on 6, 12 and 13 November 1918, are of special interest. On 6 November, he discussed his father's proposal that he – Arthur – carve a memorial plaque to Alasdair. He went on to reflect on the importance of Edinburgh and the Outlook Tower for his father and himself and concluded with a kind of health report:

> Still on the whole I'm fairly fit, and getting fitter physically and mentally. I had recognized the 'habit' of getting health in the six months or so before being called up, and health will come. I'm able for more than I was when I came, I know. (Arthur's underlining).

This shows that the Tribunal must have reconsidered their decision and that Arthur had been drafted into the forces in a non-combatant role, no doubt releasing some poor soul for service in the trenches. It also suggests that the military life had its positive side.

> From LSDP on 12 November 1918:
>
> The great news has come. We heard here about 11.30am. I expect every-one has had much the same experience on hearing – a sort of almost dazed but joyous wonder, growing to jubilation, tho' I too felt a cross-current of sorrow as the realization of peace and the end of the fighting made war seem less inevitable, with all its losses and ours. I mean we can't help feeling by contrast to the joy of those returning the loss of those who can't.
>
> Still here is the end, and the end they wished, that is the great thing. I suppose it's all for the best too, tho' before (President) Wilson appeared among our counsellors I almost feared such a victory... What of Central Europe? Of Peace in the Future?

As elsewhere, there were jollifications. Arthur got out the unused trumpets and drums, an ad hoc band – including the Sergeant Major – formed and marched round the place, 'followed by nearly all the girls'. There was free beer in the canteen and Arthur took in his fiddle 'and got 'em to dance it off'.

> At 8.oopm I wanted something quieter and... climbed a hill and saw the Cathedral towers across a gap through a wonderful strange mist. Planes overhead were turning head over heels and sending off coloured lights.
>
> The Cathedral service was 'disappointing – still!'

Much of the letter of 13 November 1918 consists of greater detail of the immediate celebration of Peace. It begins:

> Peace at last! (And everyone says 'Peace! – few Victory! Somehow the first seemed further away and victory was announcing itself as the troops advanced).

And concludes:

> I feel a little stunned by it all and hardly know what I think of things. Briefly, one looks forward to possibilities and a new world and I know I've a desire to be part of it.

Here, Arthur is speculating on how he may 'get free without further loss of time'. Already he seems to have established that his Commanding Officer is not forwarding any applications for discharge 'pending further Air Ministry Orders'.

Post-war, poor Arthur was torn between the demands of his father, who expected him to fill the shoes of both Anna and Alasdair, and his desire to complete his doctorate and build an academic career.

On a personal note, the paths of Arthur and I crossed a few times. He and I had one or two misunderstandings – not necessarily his fault – but I have one very clear memory of Arthur in operation. The place is the Geography Department of the University of Edinburgh and the time is 1962 or thereabouts. A meeting of the GeogSoc (Geographical Society) is about to take place. Arthur is to chair the meeting and is sitting alone on the platform. A servitor (yes, that was his title!) came in with the message that the speaker had called off at the last minute...

Was Arthur discomfited? This old guy being eased out by a new broom from Canada? Not one bit. He disappeared for a few minutes and came back with a big bundle of his *Songs of Ben and Glen* which he distributed among the disgruntled audience. Then he took up his fiddle and led us – bored sophisticates on the brink of Beatlemania – into an hour of good, clean, honest musical participation, sending us home genially buzzing.

Arthur's War was Sad as well as True. All around him was unhappiness and misery and unnecessary death. Mental agony and confusion must have affected him daily. His adored brother was killed, and the War most likely shortened his mother's life.

And yet, he could probably have taken some consolation from the belief that he had done some positive good for a few victims of war. In the scale of things – the first day of the Somme, for example – his contribution was probably negligible, but we can never know what, if any, difference he made. Certainly, the military service he was forced into – 'with zero to do' – did little, either for the conduct of the war or for his self-esteem.

Arthur's last home was only a few minutes' walk from Morningside Cemetery, the last resting place of many of Edinburgh's middle class. One of the gravestones commemorates one of Florence Nightingale's nurses. Her epitaph – adapted – could apply to Arthur:

'He did what he could'.

Mabel M Barker (1885–1961)

PATRICK GEDDES AND Harry Barker were born in the same year. Both spent their formative years in Perth where they attended the local Academy; both shared common interests exploring and rambling in their local neighbourhood from Kinnoull Hill to the Tay and beyond. Their career paths deviated – Harry trained as a chemical engineer and became manager of the Maxwell Brothers fertiliser plant at Silloth. However, they maintained life-long contact, and Barker assisted Geddes financially in such ventures as The Town & Gown Association.

Geddes became Mabel Barker's god-father, a task he took seriously:

> Heartily promise to stick by the wee lassie to the utmost of my power, [and] in so far as you entrust her education to me, to do my best for it. Suppose we begin at once by suggesting for her earliest playthings as soon as she is old enough to handle things some pretty stones and shells from the beach, flowers too of course, and before she is two years old to be presented with a chunk of not too wet clay (Horror shrieks Mamma, perhaps?) (no, I don't think so after all) to make mud pies and to begin the practice of *solid* thoughts [Geddes's emphasis]. I am not joking. A philosopher of my acquaintance is doing that with much effect upon his bairns.

Such statements reflected Geddes's belief that educating young Mabel in-and-about her environment was the most important aim of a 'true' education, and the sooner started, the better. His basic principle of education was 'Vivendo Discimus' – By Living We Learn. And, as Mabel remembered, Geddes put these beliefs into practice in her infancy:

> My first memory of him is one of the earliest and most vivid impressions of childhood. We walked along the sand dunes and sea-shore of the Solway. He pointed out one fascinating object after another – seaweeds, zoophytes, shells, an orange fungus glowing in his shading hands – objects he suggested for a child's museum (which was commenced forthwith).

Mabel's was a happy childhood: a born tomboy, she had liberty, with her brother, to roam, climb trees and explore derelict chemical works. Her formal education was, however, less satisfactory and her main relief from tedium came from breaks at the Geddes family home, with Norah, two years her junior, Alasdair and Arthur, and the ever-welcome holidays at Silloth with the prospect of personal rambles.

But the biggest and most welcome change came when her father sent Mabel in 1900 to Truro High School for Girls. The High School provided a varied experiential education, which was well-suited to Mabel. Academically she did well, but equally important were opportunities afforded to boarders like Mabel to enjoy the Cornish coastline, valleys and upland moors at weekends and holidays. Mabel's years at Truro were a truly formative period, leaving her convinced that learning should be 'a living dynamic process, closely related to nature and the earth'. Mabel's life-long educational credo was not a matter of book-cramming confined to the classroom and pursuing externally imposed curricula; rather, her educational framework had to be experiential in the round, firmly embedded in Regional Survey.

After school, Mabel, encouraged by her father and godfather, spent the next 12 years training to be a teacher, gaining her first degree, teaching in schools, assisting Geddes at Dundee, and acquiring a postgraduate qualification in Geography. Under Geddes's influence she concentrated on Regional Survey and experiential learning in the environment as the twin pillars of education, and her professional life was a quest for a congenial post where she could practise these.

Between teaching posts, she operated as organising secretary for Geddes, working at differing times for the Regional Survey Association, the Sociology Society and the Le Play Society. As Kenneth MacLean says in 'A troublesome assistant who will not be dismissed':

> Although she was: 'a girl of great energy and strength', endorsing regional survey was hard work: it required patience, tact, common sense, and strength of character in her dealings with PG (especially) and others. The administrative load was demanding: shoals of correspondence; coping with enquiries about membership; timing meetings to suit differing Scottish and English school holiday requirements; arranging accommodation for participants; and vainly persuading Geddes to allow participants occasional breaks.

Easter 1914 saw Mabel organising the first Conference on Regional Survey, appropriately based in Edinburgh. In Mabel's estimation, it was fitting that Edinburgh hosted the first regional survey conference. It was the site from which Geddes's teaching on the subject mainly stemmed;

programmes of civic renewal had been initiated by him in its Old Town; and the city's environmental, historical and regional context 'made it peculiarly suitable for the beginning of regional studies'. As well as lectures, discussions and field trips, evenings often included 'At Home' sessions, given by Mrs Anna Geddes with Scottish folk songs.

Within weeks, Mabel was in Dublin assisting Geddes with the Cities Exhibition and School of Civics, just as the Great War broke out. In September 1914, Norah Geddes and Mabel Barker 'celebrated' the outbreak of war by going on a walking tour in the Lake District, the high point (if that is the correct description) of which was being led by glimmering and guttering candles through 'Doves' Nest Caves' (Mabel was 'a fearless and supremely talented climber' who pioneered many new routes and carried into her professional life much of the total dedication of the top-class mountaineer). The two young women must have spent much of their holiday discussing the War, its justification, its likely outcome and whether they should have any part in it.

We are familiar with the way in which women substituted for men in the workplace so that they could go off and fight. Rudmose Brown was Lecturer in Geography at Sheffield. He had served as Geddes's assistant at Dundee and had been in the Antarctic and Spitzbergen. In January 1916 he was 'requisitioned' by the Admiralty to write handbooks on Siberia, Finland, Norway and Sweden. Mabel, therefore, became the first female Geography lecturer at Sheffield. But, as Kenneth MacLean says:

> For the ever-restless Mabel, however effective her university work, she
> felt called to aid the war effort more directly, and in April 1916 travelled
> to the Netherlands to assist with refugees.

Mabel Barker can be considered one of the Geddes family, and, like them, she was steeped in ideas of 'Peacedom'. She addressed the 1915 London meeting of the Regional Survey Association, where her idealism shone through.

For the coming generation, education for peace through regional study was the answer. Knowledge, ideally at first-hand of each occupational group, was the way forward, but Mabel conceded: 'We do not all live in favoured regions where all occupations can be studied'. Nonetheless, outdoor experiences should be encouraged, thereby making life 'much more adventurous and exciting... We want more courage and power of enduring hardships.'

While accepting that it was difficult for individuals to work-shadow (to use modern terminology) for example, a shepherd, at least something of the elements of his work, place and the dangers faced can be experienced through climbing real hills, while acknowledging that some element of risk was involved.

Similarly, not all youngsters could actually experience the activities of a hunter, but teachers could substitute role play or use literature such as Kipling's *Jungle Book* to stimulate youthful imaginations, and

> Surely one can hunt the biggest or smallest game, in exciting manner and places, with a camera. Every keen naturalist is something of a hunter, though the best of such kill but little.

Mabel had her share of tragedy, or near-tragedy. Her brother Arnold had gone to France as a sniper. As she wrote to Anna Morton:

> I suppose shades and degrees of horror don't count for much in this business – but you well understand that it is a shock to me.

More traumatic was the shattering news that he had been killed on 28 June on the Somme. Fortunately, this information turned out to be false. In fact, he had lost a lung and was repatriated to Aberdeen.

On 'a good walk up Kinnoull (and a glance at Mt Tabor)' Mabel noted that:

> Perth is very little changed by the war so far (save for wounded in the streets as everywhere) and food regulations seem beautifully non-existent! The scones and cookies are as usual.

With the recently completed Peace Palace, the Netherlands remained neutral during the Great War. Germany respected Dutch neutrality, so when Germany invaded Belgium on 4 August 1914, thousands fled to neutral Netherlands, a restless flow peaking after the fall of Antwerp.

Mabel served in the Netherlands from April 1916 until March 1917. Not only did she see at first hand the effects of war by assisting destitute Belgian refugees and internees, but these months afforded an opportunity to put into practice something of Geddes's notion of planning for 'Peacedom'.

Mabel went to the Netherlands under the aegis of the War Victims' Relief Committee of the Society of Friends – the same organization as Arthur worked with in France. It is interesting to compare the kind of work each did. Mabel's basic task was to improve the lot of Belgian refugees and internees, initially at Uden, a camp for civilian refugees sited in the less-densely populated heathland ('*Geeste*') areas of South Brabant. Although she made return visits to Uden, the bulk of her time was spent near Amersfoort, at Elizabethsdorp, a camp for the wives, children and elderly relatives of Belgian soldiers, interned close by at Zeist.

The methods by which Mabel and her co-workers assisted these refugees were threefold. First, they provided employment. Workrooms or *Zals* were established, craftwork skills were demonstrated and workers made a wide range of items: brushes, mats, shoes and slippers, baskets woven from local reeds at Uden, and woollen rugs and cushion covers produced in the female workshops at Elizabethdorp. At Uden, by way of payment, 'points' cards were given to the refugees for their end-products, which could be exchanged for goods in the camp shops. Secondly, evening classes were offered on a range of topics, including English lessons and country dancing, socials and concerts, and – not unexpectedly from a Geddesian 'disciple' – gardening classes.

Thirdly, programmes of outdoor activities were initiated, sometimes organised through newly-formed scout troops. Mabel, like Geddes,

Fig 5 Elisabethdorp Camp, Holland, June, 1916. Mabel third from right.
Williamina C Barker

approved of the opportunities that scouting offered youngsters. It was a means of developing the physical and mental life of boys through outdoor education and training in woodcraft and camping; of fostering a self-sustaining as opposed to militaristic attitude; and assisted in the promotion of citizenship. At Uden and Amersfoort, she assisted with scouting activities for boys and girls: tracking and fire-making; demonstrating cooking and camping skills; undertaking hikes through the pine forests and heather moorland; building canoes and organising swimming parties.

For Mabel, it was a fruitful period, well summed up by Jan Levi in *And Nobody Woke Up Dead*:

> She felt that she was able to give some measure of interest and happiness to the life of the refugees and to help some of the lads and lasses through their broken times, providing hope for the future.

After the Netherlands, Mabel appears to have put the war behind her. She taught at the Priory School, King's Langley, in the Chilterns, a progressive school which suited her very well till 1925, when she joined Geddes at his *Collège des Ecossais* in Montpellier. She then started her own school – Friar Row – in Cumbria. She retired after World War II, dying in Carlisle at the age of 76.

Ultimately, as for many others, war was a tragedy for Mabel; it was a conflict of attrition, a misspent application of the best scientific brains in the service of 'Wardom' rather than 'Peacedom', as revealed in this letter to Alasdair Geddes, 15 March 1915:

> It's not a deadlock but something even more terrible I'm afraid – a definite policy of 'attrition'… They are not trying to break the lines and drive them back but to wear them thin: a thing I find it horrible to realize… but I certainly do not see the conduct of this war as stupid: on the contrary it seems to me that a perfectly amazing amount of brain-power and organisation and application of all sciences has been involved… It is the more awful that that they can be brought out and co-ordinated by war and not as yet geotechnic activities.

'Geotechnics', as used by Mabel, is 'the applied science of making the earth more habitable', as Patrick and Anna Geddes tried to do in Cyprus in 1897 and Mabel herself attempted in the refugee camps.

William McKail ('Mac') Geddes (1893–1950)

FIG 6 below is a 'team photo', taken outside Mount Tabor Cottage, probably in 1912. From right to left we have Alasdair, aged 21, wearing 'the costume of our Highland forbears', Anna Morton, wife of PG and Alasdair's mother, William McKail Geddes, aged 19, son of John McKail Geddes and cousin of Alasdair, Mary, widow of John McKail Geddes, and Sandy, William McKail's older brother.

Fig 6 'Gathering of the Clan Geddes', Mount Tabor, 1912.
Alex Geddes

Looking at the two cousins, it is not too simplistic to see them as epitomising their differing backgrounds. Alasdair is quite slight and has a certain air of diffidence about him, while William, although he is probably standing on a step, is two years younger but still looks sturdy and composed. It is tempting to see in Alasdair the Old Europe, picturesque but racked by self-doubt, while William exemplifies the new Dominions, active and enterprising, soon to come to the rescue of the Old Country.

Before examining how Bill Geddes became embroiled in Europe's family squabbles, let us remind ourselves of New Zealand's part in the Great War.

Just over 100,000 New Zealanders served the British cause out of a population of a few more than 1,000,000. Of those, 16,697 were killed and 41,312 were wounded. This is an astonishing casualty rate and one that would surely be unacceptable today in anything other than an 'existential' war – which, for New Zealand, 'strategically the least vulnerable settled place on earth' and the furthest from Franz Josef and the Balkans, it was not. But – rightly or wrongly – they were loyal to the concept of empire and the old country and flooded over the oceans 'to fight and not to count the cost' on the Western Front, Gallipoli, in Palestine and Mesopotamia. Eleven Victoria Crosses were awarded to men serving in the New Zealand forces, with another seven awarded to New Zealanders serving in British or Australian units.

John McKail Geddes was older than Patrick Geddes by ten years and immigrated to New Zealand at the age of 18. Family tradition has it that he fled from Scotland to avoid being forced into the ministry. Certainly, in his voluminous correspondence with those back home, he was careful to record his church attendance and his opinion of the various preachers, while concealing that he had gone off to the gold diggings, only to confess later to his father his backsliding.

John McKail settled down in Auckland and went into the coffee and spice business, where he made his fortune. He died in 1910 when, according to Alex Geddes:

> His widow made a career out of spending and philanthropy. Two trips to Europe with five of her children staying at places like the Ritz didn't help. She bought a brand new Daimler and motored around Europe and Britain. One of the stops was at Mt Tabor.

The Geddes family took little interest in team games and sports – but over in New Zealand, William McKail (Bill, Billy, Mac) contrived to fit a successful – if short – rugby career into the immediate pre-war period. As a first five-eighth (inside centre in our terms today) or fly-half, he played regularly for the Auckland provincial team. In 1913, Auckland defeated Australia and later that year Geddes was selected for the All Blacks, who defeated Australia in a Test Match 25–13.

In the Great War, he served in the New Zealand Expeditionary Force in Egypt, France and Belgium, starting as a Second Lieutenant in the 3rd Battery, New Zealand Field Artillery, with whom he served till almost the end of the war. He was awarded the Military Cross for operations at Messines in 1917, the official citation stating:

> As Forward Observing Officer he displayed the greatest courage in reconnoitring enemy country under heavy shell fire. He sent back information of great value to his brigade, and throughout the operations his daring and resourcefulness contributed in a large degree to the success of our artillery.

Fig 7 Bill ('Mac') Geddes, MC, 1917
(Note right hand)
Alex Geddes

In September 1918, he was badly wounded and was promoted to Major while in hospital in Kent. After the war, he was managing director of the family firm and satisfied his adventurous side with sailing and speedboat racing. Between the wars he commanded the North Coast Artillery, and in 1940–41 he was Auckland fortress commander.

Bill frequently wrote home to his mother and sister. Many of these letters survive and have been transcribed by Alex Geddes. To the treasure-hunter they are rather disappointing. There are no gory descriptions of 'going over the top', or lyrical evocations of the peace after conflict, or criticisms of the top brass. There are two reasons for this. All mail, even officers', was censored and Bill was too intelligent to write something that would alarm his mother by its mutilated form. And his letter-writing was meant to reassure those at home, hence much of the content is trivial gossip and any account of action is blandly reassuring or cheerfully self-deprecating.

Yet there is much worth quoting, especially if we read between the lines. For example:

> Just a few lines before I go to sleep, that is, if sleep is possible. I am in a little dugout built by my own exertions in the trenches once occupied by Fritz but out of which we drove him a few days ago. The weather is perfect, just ideal for the business we have in hand now and of course although the enemy continues to plaster us we seem to be steadily getting him under and punishing him very severely.

> I said the weather is good, the countryside – miles behind the lines – looks fresh and green and glorious but hereabout where the fighting rages not a leaf and very few blades of grass are to be seen. Occasionally a stump of tree with one or two or part of a jagged branch stands. The villages of course are non-existent, only a few bricks scattered about.

> Our boys continue to do great work. They are a great lot and excellent fighters.

> 'An army marches on its stomach' – Napoleon.

> We are being fed pretty well in the line, and to the rations which we draw, we add what we can buy from the army canteens. But there is one item we cannot get – that is butter. For a long time past margarine has been substituted and I long for a taste of NZ *beurre*. If you could send an occasional 1 lb tin of Dairy Assn butter, it would be appreciated more than you can guess. Otherwise we fare pretty well.

Here are the first two paragraphs of a long letter sent 'from your loving soldier Bill' to Jess. One can only admire his modesty:

> What a great deal has happened since I last wrote to you. We have taken part and done well in the greatest battle of all time when brother Bill won a ribbon or more important still when the same chap went through it all as FOO for this group and still lives to tell the tale of the others who went out in the same capacity for other groups. Some don't. Most don't.

> When we came out of it and our nerves were in a pretty shaky way we were sent away to England on leave. Since I had a pretty rough spin I was

one of the first of the subalterns to go. Just fancy, Jess, being sent on leave without any warning. But I can assure you I did not miss the train.

(FOO was military speak for Forward Observation Officer, as Alasdair was, and as has been described earlier.)

In November 1917, Bill's sister Mary had been impressed by some New Zealand soldiers she had seen in Sydney, Australia where she was working for the YWCA. He replied:

> You would be more proud if you could see our little Division here. They are the real stuff too I can assure you and have got a punch that takes a lot of getting over. I'm pretty sure the old Boche knows it too for we have on a couple of occasions been up against his best and given him a sorry run.

> This year the fighting had been putting… and how grandly Britain has fought. Her effort this year has been wonderful and had Russia not let us down so badly I am sure we would have beaten the Germans completely in arms. However the war goes on and we must fight on as cheerfully as possible and as hard as we can.

Winter weather did not daunt the New Zealander:

> Winter is coming on us fast now, making this business pretty severe. But we went through the last one alright and so should have no difficulty in going through another.

After knocking Russia out of the war, whole armies were transferred to the Western Front and on 21 March 1918, the Germans attacked 'with clinical precision' and devastating success. A letter of 4 April to Bill's brother Sandy from 'Polly' has the same laconic style as one of Bill's:

> These are times of many hardships but we are doing well and four days ago I had the great pleasure as well as the unpleasantness of giving the Hun a dishing when he tried to attack our front. My Company – I have one again – did very well and although I lost 30 per cent killed and wounded, we smashed the old Hun to leg in great style.

Geddes was badly wounded in September 1918. Who better than him to describe the experience – in his inimitable, downbeat way? Letters were written on successive days to his sister and mother from No 1 New Zealand General Hospital, Brockenhurst, Hants. To provide a better narrative, I quote from the second letter first:

Here I am in a lovely comfy bed, quite the nicest, cleanest and happiest chap for miles around. I haven't been in such a fine place as this for many a long day.

It is two days now since they extracted the bullet which nearly made Bill Geddes croak his last. It entered the back of my neck and turning end over end, ploughed through to the front but as it hit up against the bone on the left side of my throat it failed to come out and so the doctors found it necessary to put me on the chopping block. The medicos lead me to believe that I am extremely lucky to be alive.

Before I got the knock I was going through the greatest experience of my life. We were getting a bit of real open warfare which we had not had in France before. My Major went away on English leave on the 18th of August and I took command of the battery 48 hours later and the big show began.

We had some rough times of course but came through very well and the old 3rd Battery did some rare shooting. The old 3rd Battery has always been the most hostile in our division and as a consequence we lose a higher percentage of officers than other batteries – but this time I'm glad to say I was the only officer wounded.

Note the almost palpable relief when he turns from the personal to the professional – as he does in this letter of 19 September:

I am getting on well. The operation passed, gave me very little trouble and the doctors and sisters look at me aghast and can't understand how it is that wound, anaesthetic and operation have had absolutely no effect on my spirits, pulse or temperature. All hands regard me as more or less of a freak. I was smoking a cigarette and playing the gramophone within half an hour of becoming conscious.

Today too when I had to go before a Board of Medical Officers instead of them inspecting me in bed I bounced into their room with a cheery good morning. They were much surprised, told me what a lucky youth I was and they congratulated the surgeon on his work. The wound was a bad one and they told me I was lucky in not going west before I was admitted to hospital. Furthermore, the operation was a delicate one, so delicate that they would not take the responsibility in France but sent me over to our own NZ people. This, of course, the doctor told me after I was out of harm's way, so you see I have every reason to feel very pleased with my double escape. There can't be much doubt that someone is looking after one old Bill Geddes. All the staff here are NZ'ers and a very good staff it is too. Or rather I should say the Doctors and Sisters are

NZ'ers while there are here also numerous English VADs and fine girls they are too. They all have to work very hard, especially just now that the NZ casualties are heavy.

I learn that at last they have taken the NZ Division out of the line for a spell and high time too. Poll (see above) has been lucky. He was on leave during the stunt and as soon as he got back to France the Division went out of the line. His battalion got a pretty rough handling too by the way.

Bill received some good news on 29 September. Again, there is no boasting, although he had, by now, had three years of active and distinguished service. What he did not know was that his tenure of his new rank was not going to be for long.

Rather good news arrived here this morning. Your old brother Bill has been promoted to the rank of Major – which is not too bad for me considering there were about 15 or 20 officers senior to me, on the gradation list, but this time however they have apparently waived the seniority aside. I will now probably go to a different battery. Get one of my own as a matter of fact. A 6 gun battery is not a bad command.

And so ended what was a 'good war' for William McKail Geddes. We started with an old photo of the Geddes cousins outside Mount Tabor Cottage, where their fathers – John McKail and Patrick – had spent their formative years. We are struck by the similarity of their military service in the Great War. Both were associated with the artillery, both served as Forward Observation Officers and both were decorated for their service in that role.

Bill enlisted before his older cousin. Alex Geddes suspects that he was just doing what many other young men were doing at that time, while Alasdair went through agonies of indecision before finally deciding to join the war effort. When he did, he had a very clear idea of what he wanted to do – in effect to be just like his cousin – and prepared accordingly. There is no evidence that Bill directly influenced Alasdair, but Alasdair would have known of Bill's exploits and seen that this was a valuable role to play, however dangerous.

Extract from *Who's Who* 1930

GEDDES, Patrick, late Professor of Sociology and Civics, University of Bombay; Professor of Botany (retired), University College, Dundee (St Andrews University); Senior Resident of Univ Hall, Edinburgh; Director of the Cities and Town Planning Exhibition; b 1854; y s of late Capt. Alex. Geddes; m 1st, 1886, Anna (d. 1917), e d of Frazer Morton, merchant, Liverpool; two s, one d; 2nd, 1928, Lilian, 2nd d. of late John Armour Brown, Moredun, Paisley. Education: Perth Academy, Royal School of Mines, University College, London; Sorbonne: University's of Edinburgh, Montpellier etc. Successively Demonstrator of Physiology at University Coll., London; of Zoology at University of Aberdeen; of Botany at Edinburgh; Lecturer on Natural History in School of Medicine, Edinburgh; with intervals of travel, eg exploration in Mexico, visits to Continental universities, zoological stations, and botanic gardens, as also to Cyprus and the East, to USA etc. *Studies*: geography, biology, history, art, social economy and civics. Educational work (besides teaching) mainly in organisation of University Halls, Edinburgh and Chelsea, each as a beginning of collegiate life, eg at Edinburgh, with its Summer Meeting and Outlook Tower. This is a regional, geographic, and synthetic type-museum, with associated undertakings of geotechnic and social purpose eg city improvement (Old Edinburgh, etc), gardens, parks etc, Publishing house (Geddes and Colleagues) associated with Celtic and general literature and art, with geography, education and synthetics. Actively occupied in city improvement, town-planning, and educational initiatives at home, on continent and in India, etc and with University designs (India, Jerusalem, etc), and development of Cité Universitaire Mediterraneanne at Montpellier. *Publications: Evolution of Sex, Evolution, Sex, Biology* and *Life in Evolution* (jointly with Prof. J. Arthur Thomson); Chapters in *Modern Botany; City Development; Cities in Evolution; The Life and Work of Sir Jagadish C Bose, FRS*, 1920; *The Coming Polity* (with VV Branford); *Ideas at War* (with Prof. Gilbert Slater); *Our Social Inheritance* (with VV Branford), etc *Recreations*: gardening, rambling. *Address*: Outlook Tower, Univ Hall, Edinburgh; c/o Sociological Society, Leplay House, 65 Belgrave Road, S.W.1; Collège des Ecossais, Montpellier, France.

Notes

1 Sri Lankan mothers frightened their children with the *Emden* 'bogeyman'. The word *emden*, meaning 'streetwise', entered the Tamil language after the successful attack on Madras. Fear of *Emden* so affected the people of the Malabar coast that 'emenden' (= great) became part of their vocabulary – although *Emden* never attacked their coast.

2 First Lieutenant Helmuth von Mücke, in command of the landing party, carried on the adventure. Having declared Direction Island a German possession, he had it fortified. He then commandeered an old and rotten schooner and took his little force through shallows and reefs to Sumatra without a chart. From Sumatra, a German merchant vessel took them to North Yemen – then in the Turkish Empire. 'An epic overland journey under constant harassment' took them to Constantinople. And so back to Germany – and a welcome for heroes! The prisoners from *Emden* were transferred to Singapore, where they helped the authorities to defend the barracks against mutineers who killed 47 British soldiers.

3 Germany, Japan, Italy and Spain withdrew in 1936. The United States never joined. Technically, the League of Nations survived until 1946, when it was replaced by the United Nations Organisation.

4 HJ Fleure (1877–1969), zoologist and geographer, best remembered today for *Human Geography in Western Europe*, *The Peoples of Europe*, *Races of England and Wales* and *A Natural History of Man in Britain*.

5 Magersfontein was a disaster in the sense that the Highland Brigade was defeated by a much smaller force of Boers, but more particularly that they were poorly led and behaved badly on the battlefield. The distress would have been compounded by the fact that the Geddeses had seen these men on parade. Major-General Wauchope, who led the Highland Brigade, was a well-known local laird, almost a cult-figure, who had distinguished himself in the Ashanti and Egyptian campaigns and had almost beaten Gladstone in his Midlothian election campaign. Wauchope was somewhat fortunate in being killed while leading his troops in the field; although Lord Methuen, who was ultimately responsible for the disaster, walked away unscathed and even made it to Field Marshal in 1911.

6 The reference is to the Bruce Bairnsfather cartoon character 'Ole Bill', who sits in his shell hole with all hell let loose around him, saying: 'Well, if you knows of a better 'ole, go to it.'

CHAPTER 2

Out of the Frying Pan

THE SIGNALMEN AT Quintinshill signal box had a nice and cosy working arrangement which made life easier for them and did no-one any harm. Quintinshill was on the main Caledonian line ('The Premier Line') from Glasgow to Carlisle, about one and a half miles north of Gretna. As well as the two main lines, one 'up' to Carlisle, one 'down' to Carstairs, there was a passing loop on either side. The signal box was not very accessible by road, so that the custom grew up of the early morning relieving signalman getting a lift on the Carlisle–Beattock local passenger train, rather than walking along the line from Gretna.

On 22 May 1915, George Meakin was on the night shift and due to finish at 6.00am. James Tinsley should have taken over at 6.00am but took the local 6.17am train from Carlisle. Express trains – running late – were approaching from either direction. The up goods loop was occupied by a train of empty coal trucks. The down loop was occupied by the 4.50am goods train from Carlisle, so the local train was shunted on to the up-line, leaving the down line clear for the 5.50am Glasgow express from London and Carlisle.

In the signal box, Meakin had scribbled down the train movements after 6.00am on a scrap of paper, and Tinsley began to enter these in the train register. The fireman from the local train should have taken certain precautions, and was in the signal box when he should have reminded Tinsley that his train was on the wrong track. Two other railwaymen – against the rules – were also in the box and were all engaged in lively discussion about the war.

The local train on the wrong line was overlooked. Various technical procedures and precautions were not carried out until, at 6.49am, an express troop train from the north, doing 70 miles per hour, burst upon the scene.

The 1/7th (Leith) Battalion of the Royal Scots was a Territorial unit based on the Dalmeny Street drill hall, with one company from the mining towns of Midlothian. After a winter guarding the shores of the Firth of Forth, they had volunteered for Foreign Service and were now on the way from their camp at Larbert, near Stirling, to Liverpool, from whence a troopship would transport them to Gallipoli, where they were sorely needed.

The phrase 'a perfect storm' has come into common currency recently, and at Quintinshill practically everything that could go wrong did go wrong, with tragic results. The troop train smashed into the stationary local train, both – as well as the goods train and coal wagons – ending up in smithereens. A minute later, before anyone could catch their breath, the Glasgow-bound express came crashing through the debris. Tinsley was probably too shaken to have done anything in time to avert or minimise this last crash but had enough presence of mind, at 6.53am, to get messages off to Gretna and Kirkpatrick, sealing off the lines and reporting the disaster. In the space of five minutes, a normal early morning scene was transformed into a hell of destruction with broken men crying and screaming in disarray.

Typically, the rolling stock of the troop train was obsolete Great Central Railway stock and mostly of wood; easily inflammable. The light-ing was by gas, stored in cylinders under the carriages, and which was now ignited by the fires from the engines. The troops had been locked into their compartments – probably to prevent desertion en route – so that they were trapped as the mass of wreckage turned into an inferno. In this new horror, men were burnt alive and some begged their comrades to finish them off. Trapped men hacked at their own limbs as they tried to free themselves from the wreckage.

There was very little water at the site for what emergency efforts could be improvised. The Caledonian Station Superintendent in Carlisle sent out a special train with doctors and all available ambulance and fire-fight-ing equipment at 7.43am. For some reason, it was not until 8.40am that the Chief Constable of Carlisle was informed of the accident and it was 8.55am before the fire engine was ordered out. It took until the following morning for the fire to finally be extinguished.

There was some heroism and quick thinking. At the rear of the troop train were ammunition wagons, and some of the soldiers unhitched these and pushed them back up the line, thus avoiding an even more complete disaster.

And disaster it was. The worst disaster in British railway history. Of the 500 soldiers who left Larbert on the troop train, only seven officers and 58 men were present at roll call at 4.00pm that afternoon. 16 civilians died. Of the troops, 83 bodies were identified, 82 were recovered but unrecognisable and 50 were completely missing. The total was agreed at 214, but, as the regimental roll was lost in the fire, this cannot be accepted with confidence.

After the roll call, at 4.30pm, the remnants of the battalion entrained for Carlisle, where they marched 'proudly' to the Castle 'amid the tears and cheers of the populace'. From there they were despatched to Liverpool by train next day to the troopship *Empress of Britain*. Just as she was about to sail, the men and one officer were medically examined and found unfit to serve overseas. They were sent back to Edinburgh. As a final indignity, on the march back to the station:

> Looking bedraggled and without much of their equipment, the men were mistaken for prisoners-of-war by Liverpool children who stoned them.

Two days after the disaster, the Royal Scots' bodies were taken back to Edinburgh. On 24 May, they were buried in a mass grave in Rosebank Cemetery. PLATE 2A. A melancholy photo of the time shows the cortege of hearses proceeding down Pilrig Street, the boundary between Edinburgh and Leith, escorted by the 15th and 16th (McCrae's Battalion) Royal Scots. These units were in training. One wonders at their thoughts as they lined the route – their turn would come. 24 May was the Queen's Birthday holiday. One *Scotsman* reader was shocked by the insensitivity of the public:

> On Monday when every heart in the city was aching and many were breaking, Edinburgh was bright with flags fluttering gaily, top mast high.

No-one had thought to lower them to half-mast. The cortege took four hours to complete its task.

As well as the Royal Scots' monument and graves, there is also in Rosebank a very small Commonwealth War Graves cemetery, with the standard memorial and eight stones – the eight graves being elsewhere in the cemetery. These fellows died between 1915 and 1921. Two of them were seamen, three from the Royal Scots and one each from the Black Watch, the Highland Light Infantry and Royal Garrison Artillery. Leith Royal Infirmary had become Leith War Hospital, and these unfortunates must have been so badly wounded that they lingered long before dying.

The legal consequences were complicated by the fact that the accident had happened in Scotland, but many of the deaths were in England. It was agreed that the signalmen should be tried in Edinburgh, where both were charged with culpable homicide and breach of duty – and found guilty. Tinsley received three years penal servitude, after which he went back to the Caledonian, and worked as a lamp-man and porter at Carlisle until he retired 30 years later. Meakin was imprisoned for 18 months and returned to the railway as a goods train guard. He was made redundant and, incredible as it may seem, set up business as a coal merchant, trading from Quintinshill siding, next to the scene of the crash. How could he face going to work every day? During the Second World War he worked in the Gretna munitions factory until he retired due to ill health.

But the mincing machine that was Gallipoli still had to be fed. The survivors of the 1/7th Royal Scots were made up to strength by drafts of other units and joined the 4th and 5th Battalions in the Dardanelles in mid-June. Thinking of perfect storms, the survivors may have said of Gallipoli, 'You ain't seen nothin' yet'.

A swift and powerful attack on Gallipoli in early 1915 was probably not a bad idea. The Dardanelles was the narrow channel through which the waters of the Black Sea poured into the Mediterranean. Turkey had been drawn into the war by Germany, and an attack through the Dardanelles could link the French and British forces with the Russians. Constantinople (as it was then) could be captured, and with one swift blow Turkey would be knocked out of the war. A British fleet had rushed the Dardanelles in 1807 and around 1906 the idea re-emerged, only to be dismissed at first.

However, in the winter of 1914–15, the Western Front was in a stalemate. The Turks' record in the Balkans in 1912–13 and at the start of the 1914 war had not been good and it was assumed they would be easily beaten. In February 1915, a naval force cleared away mines and bombarded Turkish forts. Then a combined British and French fleet of 18 old, but still serviceable, battleships attempted to clear the straits. Three of the capital ships were sunk and another three severely damaged. Thereafter the Navy took little interest in the Gallipoli venture.

Also, the element of surprise was lost. In February, the Turks had only one division in the peninsula. By April, they had three more divisions on the peninsula, and another two on the Asiatic shore.

Kitchener had predicted that 150,000 men would be needed to take Gallipoli. The Mediterranean Expeditionary Force numbered 75,000 – all that could be spared from the Western Front – in a mad scramble to get the invasion under way. Although General Sir Ian Hamilton was distrusted as being too innovative and imaginative, he had great and varied experience and had twice been recommended for the Victoria Cross – refused once because he was too young, and again because he was too old. He was appointed Commander on 12 March and the following evening left Britain.

Hamilton now became responsible for organising armed landings:

> He had no specialised landing craft, the disparate troops he had been given had no training and supplies for the army had been packed in ways which made them difficult to access for landings. Hamilton believed that the navy would make further attacks during his landings. The navy, realising likely losses and fundamentally opposing the idea that tactical losses of ships was acceptable declined to mount another attack. The Turks had been allowed two months warning from the first serious navy attack to prepare ground defences before the follow-up ground landing could be mounted, and they used the time effectively.

Hamilton's command style seems to have been to come up with a plan and leave its execution to his subordinates, retiring to the battleship HMS *Queen Elizabeth* offshore and interfering minimally in the command of battle. The terrain was hostile and the defence resolute. Losses were enormous at each of the landing beaches, and once a toehold had been gained it became a question of trench warfare as on the Western Front – but a thousand miles away from base. Water, artillery and ammunition were always in short supply and disease was rife. The plight of the wounded seemed to have changed little from the Crimea, not so far away.

Nowhere exemplifies better than Gallipoli the dichotomy between success in battle and courage. The French did not do too badly. On 25 April the 1st Lancashire Fusiliers won 'six VCs before breakfast'. Gallipoli was the forge on which the Australians and New Zealanders left behind their colonial identity and began to see themselves as nations in their own right. Anzac Day (25 April) is a major event in the Antipodean Calendar, when the 12,000 killed at Gallipoli are remembered. While 25,000 British were killed, this represented a much smaller proportion of the population.

In mid-June, the 4th and 7th Royal Scots arrived in Gallipoli as part of the 156th Infantry Brigade of the 52nd Lowland Division, finding themselves under the command of 'Hunter Bunter' (Major-General Sir

Aylmer Hunter-Weston), 'a callous, vain, bombastic and unimaginative man'.

'That will blood the pups' was his comment on the day just to be described. 'Casualties, what do I care for casualties?' was his mantra, while Paul Cowan wrote; 'The slaughters Hunter-Weston organized during his career were often the result of sheer stupidity.'[1]

On 28 June, a week after disembarkation, the Royal Scots took part in a major attack on the Turkish positions. General Hamilton blamed the inexperienced Scots for attacking without proper artillery support. Who was to blame for that? In his diary he wrote:

> The attack by the Lowland Division seems to have been mishandled. A brigade made an assault on the east of the Ravine; the men advanced gallantly but there was a lack of effective preparation.
>
> Two battalions of the Royal Scots carried a couple of the enemy's trenches in fine style and stuck to them, but the rest of the brigade lost a number of good men to no useful purpose in their push against H12.
>
> One thing is clear. If the bombardment was ineffective, for whatever cause, then the men should not have been allowed to break cover.

The Royal Scots also lost 'a number of good men'. The 4th battalion had 16 officers and 204 other ranks killed or missing, while the 7th battalion was reduced to six officers and 169 soldiers, roughly the size of a company.

A further horror has to be recorded. Wounded lay scattered about the rocky landscape, unable to be rescued. The Mediterranean scrub and grass was set on fire and swept across no man's land, where the poor wounded suffered a horrible death within earshot of their comrades. Some had survived the frying pan of Quintinshill, only to be consumed in the fire of Gallipoli. Sources differ, but when the Gallipoli Campaign ended over 100,000 men were dead, including 56,000–68,000 Turkish and around 53,000 British and French soldiers. One source gives 43,000 allies killed or missing, including 9,798 French, 1,358 Indians, 8,709 Australians and 2,721 New Zealanders, about a quarter of those who had landed on the peninsula. In total there were nearly half a million casualties during the campaign, with the British Official History listing total losses, including the sick, as 205,000 British, 47,000 French and 251,000 Turkish. Yet Turkish casualties have been disputed and were likely higher, with another source listing 2,160 officers and 287,000 other ranks. Many soldiers became sick due to the unsanitary conditions, especially from enteric fever, dysentery and diarrhoea. It is estimated that at least 145,000 British soldiers became ill during the campaign. Thirty-six Victoria Crosses were awarded, nine to Australians, 23 to British and four to Irish.

Nothing could change this saddest of stories, but let us look for something positive. Following the failure of the Dardanelles expedition, Hamilton was recalled to London on 16 October 1915, effectively ending his military career. He was replaced by General Sir Charles Monro, who contrived to extricate the Mediterranean Expeditionary Force from the peninsula, on 8 January 1916, without incurring any casualties.

Note

1   The establishment view of Hunter-Bunter differs from mine. Let me just say that he re-emerges, promoted to Lieutenant-General, as commander of VIII Corps on the Western Front. He was an engineer, yet contrived to mismanage the mining of the Hawthorn Redoubt on 1 July 1916, which was exploded ten minutes before the infantry of VIII Corps went over the top. Ten minutes was ample time for the enemy to emerge from their dugouts and bring down artillery support, so that the assault troops took the full force of the German defence. Haig described him as 'a rank amateur'. On 1 July:

> It was Hunter-Weston's divisions... that suffered the worst casualties and failed to capture any of their objectives.

CHAPTER 3

Dark Lochnagar

DESPITE THE NAME, Lochnagar is a mountain, although it has nestling under its northern cliffs and almost invisible to all but a few hardy souls a little corrie loch of that name. Lochnagar means 'Loch of the Goats', a clue to the past landscape.

The view from Invercauld over the old bridge over the Dee, with a snow-capped Lochnagar looming over the scene, is almost a photographic cliché. It has appeared in countless numbers of magazines, calendars and postcards. Lochnagar can be seen from great distances and from a score of viewpoints. Few mountains have captured emotions so powerfully as Lochnagar – and for good reason.

By British standards, Lochnagar is a big mountain. At 3,786 feet (1,155 metres) it ranks 20th in the list of Munros. Standing on the summit cairn (*Cac Carn Beag* – 'Small Shit Cairn'), looking south, there is no summit of comparable height till the *Massif Central* in France. It is a big mountain also in that it is not a pyramid like the Matterhorn but is basically a big plateau, out of which rise tops with evocative names.

The south side is quite steep, vegetated and not easy to access for climbing. The north side is quite another story, with stupendous cliffs of granite with deep gullies. Little sunshine means that this face holds the snow and ice (which suits the climbers) but also gives the Romantic title of Dark Lochnagar.

The rough granite gives good holds and this is one of the traditional playgrounds of Scottish climbing, where many great climbers learned their trade. Today's climbers are reluctant to carry their ironmongery to the start of climbs, so that Lochnagar is not as popular as it once was.

Lord Byron (1788–1824)

A mountain of character, Lochnagar has inspired local people and visitors with love and awe. The young George Gordon Byron, 6th Lord Byron was brought up in Aberdeen and was a scholar at the Grammar School till he moved on to Harrow at age ten. In his poem 'Lochnagar', the

19-year-old ultimate Romantic looks back to where his 'young footsteps in infancy wander'd'. The young Byron did not go home '… till the day's dying glory Gave place to the rays of the bright Polar star.' He sighs for the 'cataracts foam' and 'the pine-cover'd glade'.

The poem soon took on a life of its own. Very early on it must have been locally set to music and appeared as a waltz, a Schottische and a Strathspey – although 'the strathspey would be a sod to sing' (being slower than a Schottische). Beethoven made a rather florid arrangement of the poem for George Thomson in Edinburgh, the same George Thomson for whom Burns wrote or rewrote so much. There is a Dark Lochnagar kilt and 'a very fine malt whisky called Royal Lochnagar'. Prince Charles wrote a children's book called *The Old Man of Lochnagar*.

In our own time the folk group The Corries zipped up the lyric a bit to produce a very acceptable folk song.

The last four lines of Byron's poem superbly express his discontent with the pretty and bland, and his nostalgia for wild nature:

England, thy beauties are tame and domestic
To one who has roamed over mountains afar
Oh! For the crags that are wild and majestic,
The steep frowning glories of dark Lochnagar.

Queen Victoria (1819–1901)

Queen Victoria loved the Highlands, so much she made a home there and made a book from her adventures. *Leaves from the Journal of Our Life in the Highlands* was a best-seller in its time and is still a jolly good read. One of the first entries is the 'First Ascent of Loch-na-Gar, Saturday 16 September 1848'.

Albert and Victoria set off in a post-chaise to Balloch Buie, 'where our ponies and people were'. The 'people' comprised two guides 'with our luncheon in two baskets' and a groom. As usual with Victoria, she gives names and family histories of her servants – a practice which gave great offence to members of the court. The ascent took four hours, partly on foot and partly on the ponies. At two points, Albert took off in pursuit of sport. He was too late to catch some deer, but later emerged from the mist with two ptarmigan. At the top, visibility was only 100 yards: 'It was cold, and wet, and cheerless'. On the descent, the fog disappeared like magic and all was sunshine below... Most provoking! – and yet one felt happy to see sunshine and daylight again'.

Victoria's mixed day did not scar her for life as she and her consort went on to make longer and more arduous expeditions in their beloved hills.

In the North East of Scotland there is a remarkable survival of dialect ('Doric'), tradition and local culture. JC Milne (1897–1962) was part of a group of poets who helped to keep the Doric flag flying. In 'The Patriot' he displays the passion for the land of a 'Buchan loon':

Fecht for Britain? Hoot awa!
For Bonnie Scotland? Imph, man, na!
For Lochnagar? Wi' clook and claw!

The Lochnagar Mine

The front endpaper of Jack Alexander's *McCrae's Battalion* is a map which illustrates the attack of the 16th Royal Scots on 1 July 1916. It shows the trench systems in great detail which had to have names for reference. Behind the battalion were Berkshire Avenue and Northumberland Avenue. The McCraes' position reflected their origins, with Aberdeen Avenue, Monymusk Street, Scone Street and many others. Part of the British front line, 200 yards from the German front line, was Lochnagar Street.

A little-known aspect of war on the Western Front was carried on in three dimensions – underground. Miners and sappers from both sides went down as much as 30 metres and then drove tunnels up to 300 metres long under the enemy tunnels and strongpoints.

Packed with explosives, a mine would be exploded at the beginning of an assault. A huge crater would result and around it debris would pile up to a height of five metres, forming a parapet for a new strongpoint. The enemy – those left alive – would be so concussed by the violence of the explosion that they would offer no resistance to the advancing infantry.

The Lochnagar Mine started from Lochnagar Street and had two branches, with a combined charge of 28,000 kilos of ammonal.

Early on 1 July Brigadier-General Ternan watched the ground over which the attack was to take place from an observation-post... With one eye on his wristwatch he observed the approximate area where he knew mines were about to rip open the earth. The enemy-held village of La Boiselle...

had seen much underground fighting and the blowing of mines… the Germans had evacuated the position and only a few soldiers were killed.

It was a different outcome with the exploding of the Lochnagar mine to the south. A German strongpoint, *Schwaben Hohe*, was blasted to oblivion, some 350 feet of the enemy's front line just disappeared. A German officer and 35 men were taken from a dugout just beyond the damaged zone; he was able to inform of nine other dugouts in the vicinity each containing around 30 to 40 men. They have never been found. A crater 450 feet across had been created by two mines being exploded simultaneously in two separate chambers.

Brigadier-General Ternan recorded the scene:

> As the watches marked the half hour (7.28am) the two huge mines on the flanks of La Boiselle exploded with a concussion that shook the ground for miles around and the attack began. The mine on the right (Lochnagar) had been charged with 30 tons of ammonal, and that on the left with 20 tons, so that the effect of the explosions was terrific. The bottom of the valley was quickly obliterated from our view from the dust thrown up and the countless shells, so that one could see little or nothing except the movement of the companies of the reserve Brigade as they went forward.

In fact, the Commanding Officer of the 15th Royal Scots complained that the

> Blowing of the mine… had no effect whatsoever on the German defenders, but utterly ruined our advance.

By midday, the situation was stable from the German point of view. Apart from a few men hanging on to the lip of Lochnagar crater, the British were back in their own lines. The attack had not been a surprise, and the large distance the attackers had to cover before reaching the German front line ensured failure. It certainly hadn't helped that the attackers were loaded down with equipment and ordered to walk.

Fast forward now to 17 December 1923. The war was over and the survivors of McCrae's Battalion had raised enough money to pay for a memorial plaque in the High Kirk of St Giles. They assembled in George Street and marched up to Parliament Square. The psalm 'God is our refuge and our strength' was sung. The Regimental Colour was handed over to the Church for safe keeping. The tablet was unveiled. There were speeches.

The cult of the heroic piper really started in October 1895, with Piper Findlater winning the vc when the Gordon Highlanders stormed the Heights of Dargai on the North-West Frontier. Wounded in the ankles, he crawled to his pipes, couched himself against a rock and began playing 'in the face of a terrible fire'. As Findlater himself said:

> It was a wonder I got away with my life, for I was sitting right in the open, and the bullets were glancing around me in all directions.

In the Great War, Piper Laidlaw of the King's Own Scottish Borderers Association, at Loos, earned himself the vc when he:

> With absolute coolness and disregard of danger, mounted the parapet, marched up and down and played his company out of the trench.

So many pipers tried to emulate Pipers Findlater and Laidlaw that more than 500 pipers were killed and another 600 wounded. The War Office banned such conspicuous and wasteful gallantry – but it still went on.

So, in St Giles, as the final blessing echoed from the pulpit, Pipe Major Willie Duguid – who had first seen action at the Heights of Dargai – piped up 'Dark Lochnagar'.

And, as the tears were dabbed away, a lone bugler sounded the 'Last Post' followed by 'Reveille', as the ghosts of the battalion stood at ease.

The Scottish Mountaineering Club have a *Hillwalker's Guide to the Munros*, with an excellent winter photograph of the north-east corrie of Lochnagar. The sky is blue and there is a blanket of fresh, pure, snow overall – except for the great cliffs, where the rock shows through the ice.

In the foreground is a lone climber, perhaps overcome with emotion as he contemplates the majesty of the mountain or the vastness of geological time.

Contrast the beauty of the solitude with the sordid reality of 'Man's inhumanity to man'.

CHAPTER 4

The First Hundred Thousand

AROUND 1948, when I was a teenager, I came across the novels of Ian Hay. They were light, amusing and romantic, yet they explored all those things that bothered someone of that age. As a teenager does, I tried to read all that Ian Hay had written, and had great satisfaction when I discovered *The First Hundred Thousand*. Not only was it well written and interesting, it was thoroughly Scottish.

I had a grievance (and still have) that the Scots had contributed twice as many, pro-rata, to the conflict of the Great War as the rest of the British Isles and, for Scotland, the butcher's bill was twice as heavy, per thousand. I felt we did not get the recognition we deserved.

Fig 8 The First Hundred Thousand – Frontispiece
The First Hundred Thousand

Yet here we had a book by a recognisably Scottish Ian Hay, describing the 15 months between the recruitment of the Several (Service) Battalion of the Bruce and Wallace Highlanders – 'one of the most famous regiments in the British Army' – and the Battle of Loos.

Later, I learnt that 'Ian Hay' was a pseudonym used when he was a teacher at Fettes; no doubt, like Sir Walter Scott, reluctant to reveal to snobbish Edinburgh that he was making money from writing popular novels. In real life, he was John Hay Beith – still satisfyingly Scottish.

Even later, I discovered that he was born in Manchester (of Scots descent), was educated at Fettes and Oxford, and taught at Fettes till 1912, when he became a full-time writer. He served in the Argyll and Sutherland Highlanders (based in Stirling, as were Bruce and Wallace) and the Machine Gun Corps. He made it to Major, won the Military Cross at Loos (not mentioned in the book) and was Mentioned in Dispatches.

The Battle of Loos was fought between 25 September and 14 October 1915 and was the biggest battle of that year. The book was published later that year, so that it must have been written almost as the events described were occurring. Its freshness and topicality made it a great success.[1] There were two sequels and Ian Hay found himself in Washington with the information bureau of the British War Mission. The cover of the American edition of The First Hundred Thousand claimed that it was 'the greatest book of the War'.

Resuming civilian life he returned to his accessible literature mode, amassing novels and plays, often collaborating with such as PG Wodehouse, AEW Mason and Edgar Wallace.

During the Second World War he re-enlisted, was made Director-General of Public Relations at the War Office and promoted to Major-General – surely the only successful author (apart from memoirs and autobiographies) of general rank since Lew Wallace, the Union general, wrote Ben-Hur in 1880.

Two months into the Great War, it was clear that the struggle would not be over by Christmas. The original British Expeditionary Force (the Kaiser's 'contemptible little army') and the regulars hastily brought back from the outposts of empire had been whittled away – as had the Territorials. The war of movement of August 1914 had crystallised into a continuous line of defences from Switzerland to the North Sea, making anything other than a toe-to-toe slogging match impossible. We were in for a long haul. As Barbara Tuchman writes in August 1914:

> The nations were caught in a trap, a trap made during the first thirty days
> out of battles that failed to be decisive, a trap from which there was and
> has been, no exit.

Surely the most potent image of the Great War must be the recruiting poster of Kitchener, with his hypnotic eyes reminding us that 'Your country needs you.' On tea towels and mugs, copied and parodied in many nations 'this molten mass of devouring energy' shames us into coming forward.

Lord Kitchener was an engineer, unlike the cavalrymen who made up most of the top brass in the British army. This explains a lot. In 1914, as Secretary of State for War, he correctly predicted a long war that would last at least three years, require huge new armies to defeat Germany, and suffer huge casualties before the end would come. Kitchener stated that the conflict would plumb the depths of manpower 'to the last million'. Not only could he foresee the future, he had the capability to prepare for it,

> Organising the largest volunteer army that Britain, and indeed the world, had seen and a significant expansion of munitions production to fight Germany on the Western Front.

These were the 'New Armies'. Of Kitchener's achievement, the Cabinet Secretary of the time wrote:

> The great outstanding fact is that within 18 months of the outbreak of the war, when he had found a people reliant on sea-power, and essentially non-military in their outlook, he had conceived and brought into being, completely equipped in every way, a national army capable of holding its own against the armies of the greatest military Power the world had ever seen.

'The First Hundred Thousand' were, of course, the first wave of the New Armies, and Ian Hay's book was, in effect, what the Germans call a Bildungsroman – a tale of growing up, ending with the achievement of maturity. The author was not buzzed in from London, given a swift walk in a trench and sent back to write his column in a great national newspaper. He was there, in the thick of it – a participant observer. His First Hundred Thousand may, or may not, be a Sad Story, but it must be very close to being a True one.

The First Hundred Thousand opens with a poem.

The Dramatis Personae are assembled. The Colonel is a 'dug-out' – a fortnight ago he was fishing in the Garry. Two of his company commanders were commandeered while on leave from India 'and the other two have practised the art of war in company with brother Boer'. Three subalterns came from the Second (regular) Battalion, having been left behind earlier, and four from the Officers' Training Corps:

There are happy careless souls, like McCleary and Hogg. There are conscientious but slow-moving worthies, like Mucklewame and Budge. There are drunken wasters. There are simple-minded enthusiasts. There are the old hands, versed in every labour-saving (and duty-shirking) device. There are the feckless and muddle-headed. There is another class, which divides its time between rising to the position of sergeant and being reduced to the ranks. Another group knows the drill-book backwards but cannot handle so much as a sentry-group. There are men with initiative but no endurance, and others with endurance but no initiative.

Yet the great sifting and sorting machine gets to work to sort them all out into their appointed places. The efficient and authoritative rise to non-commissioned rank. The quick-witted and well-educated find employment on the Orderly Room staff, or among the scouts and signallers. The handy are absorbed into the transport, or become machine-gunners. The sedentary take posts as cooks or tailors or officers' servants. The waster hews wood, draws water and empties swill-tubs. The great, mediocre, undistinguished majority merely go to stiffen 'the rank and file'.

Killick lived softly and drove a Rolls-Royce for a Duke. He now was a machine-gun sergeant and a very good one. Private Mellish enlisted as 'an actor', but in his native Dunoon he followed 'the blameless but monotonous calling of a cinematograph operator'. 'In the barrack-room his manners never fell below the highest standard'. 'For such an exotic there could be only one destination' and in due course Cyril became an officer's servant:

McOstrich was a phenomenon. A dour, silent, earnest specimen, he kept himself to himself. He never smiled. He was not an old soldier, yet he performed like a veteran the very first day he appeared on parade. He carried out his orders with solemn thoroughness. He did not drink. He did not swear. His nearest approach to animation came at church. He was not a Scotsman at all, although five out of six of his comrades would have put him down as such. Altogether he was a man of mystery.

In the barrack room Private Burke of D Company, a cheery soul, made a contemptuous and ribald reference to the Ulster Volunteers, at which McOstrich crossed the floor in three strides 'and silently felled the humourist to the earth'.

Ian Hay's comment is:

Plainly, if McOstrich comes safe through the war, he is prepared for another and grimmer campaign.

Grimmer? Than the Great War? Sadly, McOstrich did not make it through the second day at Loos, where he was the first to go down.

Private McSnape was 'of the true scout breed'. He had been a Boy

Scout of no mean repute. He was clean in person and courteous in manner. He could be trusted to deliver a message promptly. He would light a fire in a high wind with two matches and provide himself with a meal of sorts where another would have starved. He could distinguish an oak from an elm.

In a night exercise, when C and D Companies were to make a surprise attack on the enemy – A and B Companies – it was McSnape who pierced the sentry-groups of the enemy's position and dismantled their trip-wire system. C and D surprised the defenders and McSnape was duly made up to lance-corporal.

Not all the Highlanders were heroes in the making. Private Dunshie had been a street news-vendor and 'the sight of work made him feel faint'. He volunteered for service as a scout, but a single experience of night operations in a dark wood scared him out of his wits. In the kitchen he prospered exceedingly until he was caught in the act of washing his hands in ten gallons of B Company's soup.

Next, Dunshie joined the machine-gunners because he had heard rumours that these were conveyed to and from their labours in limbered wagons. He soon learned that it was the guns that were carried; the gunners invariably walked, sometimes carrying the guns and the appurtenances thereof. Regimental transport came next – there was a shortage of drivers. On the first day he had to walk behind a wagon for fourteen miles, applying the brake when necessary. Next day he cleaned the stables. On day three, he was instructed on how to groom a mule. On day four, the mule – kicked him in the stomach. On day five, he was returned to his company.

But Mecca was at hand. Each company had to provide a chiropodist. (Boots and feet were – rightly – an obsession with the army). Dunshie volunteered, without knowing what a chiropodist was.

'Crime' is the subject of Chapter 5 and describes the operation of the lowest 'court' of the Army, Company Commander's Orders. The 'crimes' are banal enough and Captain Blaikie dispenses justice with a light hand and morale-building exhortation – until Private McQueen is wheeled in. Private McQueen is an unpleasant-looking creature. His misdemeanours are recited. After the corroborative evidence, Captain Blaikie says: 'I am going to ask the Commanding Officer to discharge you.' There is nothing homely or paternal in his speech now.

Go home and explain that you were turned out of the King's Army
because you weren't worthy of the honour of staying in.

With our wisdom of hindsight and greater knowledge of the world we
may look at the fate of Private McQueen and wonder – Was he just
working his ticket? What happened next? Did McQueen re-enlist under
another name and perform great deeds of heroism? Or did he enter that
shady underworld of deserters and criminals we never hear about? And
did he look up the casualty lists in the papers and spot the names of his
former mates? Shakespeare, in the great speech he gives King Harry
before Agincourt, says:

> And gentlemen in England, now a-bed
> Shall think themselves accurs'd they were not here,
> And hold their manhoods cheap whiles any speaks
> That fought with us upon Saint Crispin's day.

Did McQueen hold his manhood cheap when he heard of the slag heaps
of Loos? Or did he think: 'I did well getting out of that lot'?

Most reminiscences of the Great War rail against the ineptness of the
organisation and the vast distance – social and in terms of miles – between
the top brass and the PBI in the front line.

When the new recruits assemble for the first time there are no uniforms
– 'even their instructors wear bowler hats or cloth caps' – to say nothing
of such essentials as rifles, ammunition or bayonets. But all that is necessary for military life is gradually brought together, sometimes in the
correct order.

'Olympus' is the chapter on organisation, Hay divides Olympus into
three departments:

1 Round Game Department (including Dockets, Indents and all
   official correspondence)
2 Fairy Godmother Department
3 Practical Joke Department, and gives illuminating and hilarious
   examples from each.

> En route to the front they sat down to await the arrival of the other half
> of the regiment – which had left England many hours before them, and
> had not been seen or heard of since.

They had to wait exactly ten minutes. 'Some Staff – what?' as the Adjutant observed, as the train lumbered into view.

The officers' attitudes are cheerful, when many would be cynical. There are real nurses, undergoing drudgery and discomfort. Then there is the young person who believes that nursing is a thing of fashion.

These girls will play the angel-of-mercy game for a week or two and then jack up and confine their efforts to getting hold of a wounded officer and taking him to the theatre.

With reference to the top brass:

> We are much harried by generals at present. They roam about the country on horseback, and ask company commanders what they are doing.

On one occasion, the battalion is beset with three of these gentlemen – each with his own priorities and prejudices. All day the battalion is kept alert as they change formation, unlace their boots and generally mess around.

How reliable is Ian Hay as a historical source?

Private McSlattery had had problems accepting the necessities of military life – saluting officers, having to turn up for work every day, keeping sober and objected upon principle to have to present arms to a motor-car standing two hundred yards away upon his right front.

The great car rolled smoothly... and came to a standstill... There descended a slight figure in khaki. It was the King – the King whom Private McSlattery had never seen.

For a moment – yea, more than a moment – keen Royal eyes rested upon Private McSlattery, standing like a graven image, with his great chest straining the buttons of his tunic.

Then a voice said, apparently in McSlattery's ear: 'A magnificent body of men, Colonel. I congratulate you.'

Then there were three cheers for His Majesty the King, whereupon McSlattery shouted: 'Yin mair, chaps, for the young leddy.'

Just before the Big Push, Captain Blaikie is reflecting that he can't say he has ever noticed Staff Officers crowding into the trenches ('as they have a perfect right to do') at four o'clock in the morning when two figures, in the uniform of the Staff, become visible in Orchard Trench, picking their steps amid the tumbled sandbags, and stooping low to avoid gaps in the ruined parapet. The sun was just rising behind the German trenches.

One of the officers was burly and middle-aged and he did not appear to enjoy bending double. His companion was slight, fair-haired, and looked incredibly young. Once or twice he looked over his shoulder, and smiled encouragingly at his senior.

The pair emerged through the archway into the main trench, and straightened their backs with obvious relief. The younger officer – he was a lieutenant – noticed Captain Blaikie, saluted him gravely, and turned to follow his companion.

Captain Blaikie did not take his hat off, as he had promised. Instead, he stood suddenly to attention, and saluted, in return keeping his hand uplifted until the slim, childish figure had disappeared round the corner of a traverse.

It was the Prince of Wales.

Shakespeare tells us that, the night before Agincourt, Henry v mingled incognito among his demoralized troops and lifted their spirits. Was the Prince's visit 'a touch of Harry in the night?' Next day the King magnificently addresses his army:

> We few, we happy few, we band of brothers.
> For every man who fights today will be my brother.

McSlattery's swollen chest surely meant that he had joined a band of brothers.

Were the Argylls really favoured with two royal visits during Ian Hay's time with them? Or are they included as a dramatic necessity? What is certainly true is that, in the early part of the war, the Prince of Wales did behave in this satisfactory fashion: it was only when he got bored that he retreated to the fleshpots of Paris and the ministrations of his mistress.

Just occasionally, Ian Hay abandons the light touch for a note of high seriousness.

> Today each of us was presented with a small metal disc. Bobby Little examined his curiously.
> 'What is this for?' he asked.
> Captain Wagstaffe answered.
> 'What is it for then?'
> 'It's called an Identity Disc. Every soldier on active service wears one.'
> 'Why should the idiots put one's religion on the thing?' inquired Master Cockrell, scornfully regarding the letters 'C of E' upon his disc.

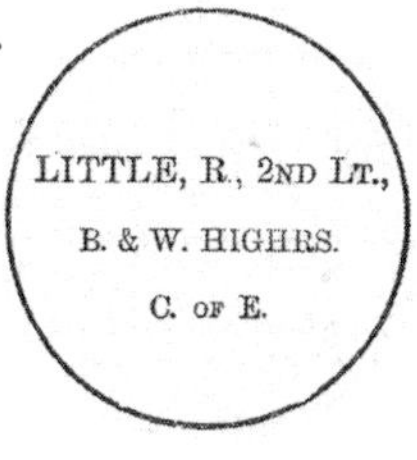

LITTLE, R., 2ND LT., B. & W. HIGHRS. C. OF E.

Fig 9 Bobby Little's Identity Disc
The First Hundred Thousand

Wagstaffe regarded him seriously.

'Think it over,' he suggested.

Peter Carmichael was one of the first to enlist in the regiment – and the first to die. 'Wee Pe'er' was underage (as transpired later), undersized, unmuscular, and extraordinarily clumsy. He was not left-handed, he was equally incompetent with either hand.

But he possessed the one essential attribute of the soldier. He had a big heart. He was keen. His kit was without blemish. For him, a merry heart went all the way. He revelled in muddy route-marches, and invariably provoked and led the choruses. The men adopted him as a sort of company mascot.

Time passed. His conduct sheet was blank, but Peter was 'ower wee for a stripe' – but his chance would come later, when he had filled out a little and got rid of his cough.

Brigade Training was set in thick woods, when heavy rain gave way to a biting east wind. An elaborate night operation ended in chaos. A whole battalion got lost without any delay or difficulty whatsoever. The other three battalions stood waiting for two and a half hours and all got home to bed, soaked and freezing at 3.00 am – with the promise that the operation would be continued at nightfall.

Fourteen of the more quick-witted spirits of A Company hurriedly paraded before the Medical Officer and announced that they were 'sick in the stomach.' Seven more discovered abrasions on their feet, and proffered their sores for inspection, after the manner of Oriental mendicants. One scrimshanker, rather ingeniously, assaulted a comrade in arms and was led away, deeply grateful, to the guard-room.

Wee Peter, who last night had stumbled into an old trench half-filled with ice-cold water and had a temperature of a 102 (had he known it), paraded with his company at the appointed time. The company, he reflected, would get a bad name if too many men reported sick at once.

Next day, he was absent from parade. He was 'for Cambridge'. (The great military hospital in Aldershot.) He made a great fight. Although his heart was big enough, his body was too frail. As they say on the sea, he was over-engined for his beam.

And so, three days later, the simple soul of 2754 Carmichael, A Company, was transferred, on promotion, to another company – the great Company of Happy Warriors who walk the Elysian Fields.

The Army honours its dead. The company was specklessly turned out and standing to attention. The firing party stood with arms reversed – 'hands upon the butt-plate and heads bowed, as laid down in King's Regulations'. The bearers placed the coffin upon the gun-carriage. Upon the lid was a very dingy glengarry, a stained leather belt, and a bayonet, but these were paid as much reverence as would be the baton and cocked hat of a Field-Marshal for they were 'the insignia of a man who has given his life for his country'.

The pipes break into a lament, a wreath from each company is laid upon the coffin.

They slow march up the hill towards the military cemetery. Each foot seems to hang in the air before the drums bid each to put it down.

Twice more the rifles ring out. Eight buglers come to the 'Ready'. Then 'Last Post', the requiem of every soldier of the King, swells out, sweet and true.

All has been done in good order and with military discipline. The chaplain closes his book. Old Carmichael finds Captain Blaikie's hand waiting for him. He grips it and says, 'Weel the laddie's had a grand sojer's funeral. His mother will be pleased to hear that.'

The old gentleman sets off down the station road. The company falls in, and we march back to barracks, leaving Wee Pe'er – the first name on the battalion Roll of Honour – alone in his glory beneath the Hampshire pines.[2]

As the Big Push neared, the mood darkened further. Moving up to the line,

> The grim realities of war are coming home to us. Outside this farm stands a tall tree. Not many months ago a party of *Uhlans* [crack German cavalry] arrived here, bringing with them a wounded British prisoner. They crucified him to that self-same tree, and stood around him till he died. He was a long time dying.
>
> Some of us had not heard of *Uhlans* before. These have now noted the name, for future reference – and action.

In the forward trench, Ian Hay meditates on the previous winter:

> Let us bare our heads, then, in all reverence, to the memory of those ... legions which saved us from utter extinction at the beginning.

The infantryman is no party to the Great Plan. As a result, the great Battle of Loos, from 25 September to 14 October, the biggest battle of 1915, in which 59,427 British and empire troops were killed, for the Highlanders boiled down to the Battle of the Slag-Heaps. Looking over no man's land, the objective was the village of Douvrin and the main hazards the mighty Hohenzollern Redoubt and Fosse 8, a coal-bing which looked 'as big as North Berwick Law'.

Even a small incident like this is incredibly complicated and unravelling the next three days is hardly necessary – we have seen something like it dozens of times. The Highlanders fought their way forward – too far forward – as the regiments on either side faltered or failed as 'the Hun' counter-attacked. 'The wily Teuton' risked no frontal attack, seeing that he could gain all his ends from the left flank. Presently Major Kemp (the Colonel having been wounded) passed the order: 'Highlanders, retire to the trenches behind, by companies, beginning from the right.'

After 72 hours fighting, the Highland Division was relieved to sleep the sleep of exhaustion in dug-outs behind a railway line and to receive, on their awakening, the thanks of the Corps Commander.

Ian Hay's last word was written three weeks later. He took leave of *The First Hundred Thousand* and suggested that someday, if Providence willed, the tale would be resumed. (In fact, *Carrying On* was published in 1917 and *The Last Million* in 1918.)

> But the title of the story will have to be changed. The sturdy valiant legions, will always be the First; but, alas! they are no longer
>
> ### The Hundred Thousand.

Notes

1 The foundation for the book was a series of articles written for *Blackwood's Magazine*. While this helps to explain the remarkable speed with which the book was published, it in no way diminishes the authenticity of Hay's account of the Highlanders' experiences.

2 Sentimental tosh or History as wished for? Surely Ian Hay has over-indulged himself over one simple private? Up till May 1915 there were over 20,000 Highlanders – Gordons, Seaforths, Argylls, Camerons and their support units – stationed in and around Bedford. Infectious disease has always been a problem for armies. By the end of January 1915, 529 had been diagnosed with measles alone. 28 of the Camerons died and at least as many were discharged. By the time the Highland Division left for France, 135 had died from illness.

CHAPTER 5

McCrae's Battalion – Eponymous or Anonymous?

EDINBURGH NOW HAS a splendid new tramline running from the airport to the city centre. The observant traveller will notice the Haymarket, where five roads converge outside the fine main line station of 1840. In the centre is a plain but imposing monument, surmounted by a handsome clock. PLATE 2B This is the memorial to those from the Heart of Midlothian Football Club who fell in the Great War.

On Wednesday 25 November 1914, 11 Hearts players enlisted and five were rejected on health grounds. They were followed by players from 75 football clubs, great and obscure. The Roll of Honour contains 42 names. Of these, 15 served in the same unit – McCrae's Battalion.

In the High Kirk of St Giles, on Edinburgh's ancient High Street, there is a memorial plaque 'in a dark interior wall' which has 'turned out to be like storing it in a dusty old attic'. This was placed there by the survivors of the 16th Battalion of the Royal Scots, the First of Foot, 'Pontius Pilate's Bodyguard' – in which 15 of those on the Hearts monument served.

Why are there two monuments in one city to the same people? And why is one bigger, better and more in the public eye than the other? Tynecastle, the Hearts ground, is accessed from Haymarket and local patriotism ensured that, during the construction of the tramway, the memorial was dismantled, stored and re-erected as a community focus. (Although it also has to be said that, latterly, the annual Armistice Day remembrance seemed to have been forgotten).

In the first month of the Great War, the British Expeditionary Force of regulars and Territorials was almost driven into the sea and it was clear that desperate measures had to be taken if it was to survive. On 28 August 1914, Field Marshal Kitchener, Secretary of State for War called for 100,000 men to volunteer. In a wave of war fever, recruiting figures broke all records and new units were formed, attached to existing regiments. They were often known as 'Pals' battalions, since those who volunteered together were assured that they would serve together in the same battalion.

In the general mess after the Great War, the Pals faded from the collective memory until Peter Whelan wrote a stage play called *The Accrington Pals*, which was premiered by the Royal Shakespeare Company on 10 April 1981. Almost simultaneously Alan Bennett wrote *One Fine Day*, a moving television play, with a typically solid performance by Brian Glover, Barnsley's best-known Thespian.

Barnsley provided two Pals battalions and Roni Wilkinson of the *Barnsley Chronicle* wrote them up in a tabloid supplement. In the autumn of 1982, the story was serialized in broadsheet form in the 'big paper'.

Sir Nicholas Hewitt, owner of the *Barnsley Chronicle* – whose grandfather had helped to raise the Barnsley Pals and became the Commanding Officer of the 13th Battalion, York and Lancaster Regiment – commissioned Jon Cooksey to write *Barnsley Pals*. Fully researched, it sold out quickly, was taken up by schools and colleges, and was used by guides to the battlefields and public speakers.

The publishers, Barnsley Chronicle Ltd, had tapped a rich seam and, in quick succession, Pals books appeared for Accrington, Sheffield, Liverpool, Leeds, Salford, Manchester, Birmingham, Hull, Swansea, and Bradford. Tyneside had two, for the Tyneside Scottish and the Tyneside Irish. In all, the histories of 40 Service battalions were covered. As a result, the detailed service history of over 100,000 men is available in readable and well-illustrated form.

The biggest day in the history of the Pals was 1 July 1916, the first day of the Battle of the Somme and the bloodiest day in the history of the British Army.

'T' best book on 't soobject' is Roni Wilkinson's *Pals on the Somme 1916* (Pen and Sword Books Ltd; Barnsley; 2006), which is detailed, authoritative and well-illustrated with anecdotes, maps and photographs.

Unfortunately for us, and given the North of England provenance of interest in the Pals, the 16th Battalion, Royal Scots ('McCrae's Battalion') scarcely rates a mention, except as a component of 34th Division. Yet on 1 July, 31 per cent of the strength was killed which should have been included as number 11 on the list of battalions suffering more than 500 casualties – next to the Accrington Pals, who have 11 entries in the index.

Fortunately, we have Jack Alexander. He found that virtually all the battalion's records had been destroyed and that none of Edinburgh's many museums, libraries or archives seemed to hold a single item. From this slender base he worked for 12 years to produce probably the best record there is of a Service Battalion – *McCrae's Battalion: The Story of the 16th Royal Scots* (Mainstream Publishing Company Ltd; Edinburgh; 2003). I have used this systematically and extensively, confident that it is of scholarly quality but still readable. In what follows, the facts may be regarded as essentially true. The opinions are my own, and may be debatable.

George McCrae (1861–1928) was the illegitimate son of Jane Buchan, resident housemaid in the home of James Nicol, Professor of Natural History at Aberdeen. Having been dismissed from her position, she (and her child) moved to a 'single end' in Arthur Street, one of the poorest areas in Edinburgh, where Jane's uncle lived. There, young George shared a bed with two young cousins.

He attended the Heriot Trust school in Davie Street,[1] leaving before he was ten 'to add to the household resources'. He was apprenticed to the Edinburgh branch of a Dunfermline hatters. At 16 he was 5ft 9 inches, looked 21, and was put in charge of the main shop in Dunfermline. At 17, he was brought back to the Edinburgh shop and joined the Edinburgh Rifle Volunteers. At 19 he set up business for himself in the Grassmarket.

McCrae was innovative and successful in business. At 27, he was promoted to Captain in the Volunteers. Next year, he stood for election to the City of Edinburgh Council. A fine public speaker, he shone from his first meeting and was unanimously elected (at 29) Treasurer to the city. In three years, he sorted out the city's massive financial problems and set in motion a range of public works. (He laid the foundation stone of the reconstructed crumbling North Bridge.)

In 1898, he opened a new branch – which became his flagship – in Princes Street and the following year was elected to Parliament. Again, he was a great hit and was brought into the Liberal establishment.

In military matters, he was promoted to Colonel and appointed to command the 40th Edinburgh Rifle Volunteers, which, under the 1907 Territorial Forces Act, became the 6th Battalion Royal Scots (TF). He was consulted regularly by Haldane, Secretary for War when, 'as the most respected Volunteer officer in the country', he was a persuasive advocate for change. For his services to Edinburgh and to Volunteering he was knighted in 1908.

Blocked by fiercely conservative institutions such as the Civil Service and the House of Lords, he accepted the chairmanship of the Local Government Board – whose remit was public health and housing.

At the outbreak of the Great War, Sir George (now 53) remained a civilian but was appointed chairman of the Scottish committee for the relief of wartime distress.

After three months of war, Sir George had a dilemma. He wanted to raise a battalion. But how could he send men to their deaths while his age protected him? A letter to the War Office offered to raise a battalion so long as he was allowed to lead it in the field, to share the risks and discomfort with his men and to die – if he had to – by their side.

On Thursday 19 and Friday 20 November the *Evening Dispatch* and *The Scotsman* carried a big story. Sir George McCrae had volunteered for the Army. He was to raise and command a battalion in the field. The city was alive! At 4.00 pm, he emerged in uniform from the door of 125 George Street to loud applause. He announced that recruiting would begin on 27 November with a grand public meeting. It would take seven days:

'Seven days?' An unbelieving murmur rose from the crowd.

'Seven days! Sir George repeated, with a broad smile.

The Usher Hall was packed. 'Patriotic ladies' queued to get out, to make space for the young men unable to get in. Sir George could handle crowds, with techniques he had learned in his hatting business. Melrose – the tea merchant in Princes Street – had installed a giant thermometer, to record progress. The platform party included the Hearts players who had signed up two days previously. There were speeches and the pipes and brass of the 4th, 6th and 9th Royal Scots struck up 'Rule Britannia'. '60 brave fellows' wanted to enlist on the spot, so there had to be an appeal from the chair for a doctor to carry out the necessary medical examination.

The pipes struck up 'Scots Wha Hae', for which the *Evening Dispatch* had printed new words:

> Who would bear a sword unsheathed?
> While the guilty Kaiser breathed?
> Rise wi' vengeance steeled and teethed,
> Strike wi' George McCrae.
> Who for Britain's realm would stand,
> Fechtin' bravely man tae man?
> Freeman rise, and in the van
> Gang wi' George McCrae.

McCrae started his speech – 'This is not a night for titles', and went on to say that – 'It is my intention that this unit will reflect accurately all the many classes of this famous capital.'

He concluded thus:

> Furthermore, with the agreement of the authorities, I have undertaken to lead the battalion in the field. I would not – I could not – ask you to serve unless I share the danger at your side. In a moment I will walk down to Castle Street and set my name to the list of volunteers. Who will join me?

And off he went, out the door and down the hill. By midnight nearly 300 men had enlisted. By Monday morning 520 men had come forward. There were 400 applications for 30 commissions. More professional footballers from other clubs came in. At Inverleith Park, eight members of an amateur side, still in their football strips, marched. 20 senior students from Broughton Higher Grade School, led in by their bespectacled mathematics teacher Peter Ross.[2]

On the next Saturday, Hearts were to play Hibs (Hibernian) in the local derby match at Tynecastle. Free admission was granted to all who had signed up. Sir George led his men in, and at half-time they marched round the touchline where several new volunteers joined in.

Mobilisation was at noon on 15 December. The volunteers assembled and marched off to the specially composed tune of 'Sir George McCrae' – on sale at a penny per sheet, proceeds to regimental funds.

We can pass over 1915, the details and fatigue of training, and move to 10 January 1916 when the battalion arrived in France. They were not expected and spent the first few days marching around, and in a grossly overcrowded train. One day, there was no breakfast, no lunch, no food at all. In due course, the 16th, the 15th Royal Scots, the Lincolns and the Suffolks came together and the 101 Brigade of the 34th Division was complete.

From 27 January to 25 February, McCrae's went up into the line, in a quiet sector where inexperienced troops could serve their apprenticeship. A second spell at the front started on 4 April. There followed three weeks of Divisional training in 'rifle, bomb and bayonet'. The 5th of May to 1st June saw another spell in the front line and a short spell in reserve. Then it was back to the front line on 15 June, ready for the 'Big Push' on 1 July.

Vast amounts have been written – of very varied quality – on this, the bloodiest day in the British Army's history. At a horrific cost, the Army made a few gains, but these were mainly retaken by the Germans. What went wrong? There were macro-reasons which bedevilled the whole operation, and micro-reasons which affected the McCraes and the regiments on either side of them.

The Germans and the French were locked into a titanic struggle for Verdun and it was necessary for the British to launch a major diversionary attack to relieve the situation. The Fourth Army commander, Lieutenant General Sir Henry Rawlinson, drew up a complex plan for an advance on an 18-mile front towards shallow objectives, preceded by a massive artillery bombardment.

The Commander in Chief, General Sir Douglas Haig, revised the plan to include deeper infantry objectives and the eventual plan was an unfortunate mixture of boldness and caution.

No more guns were available for the new plan and there was not enough ammunition to support both bombardments. Throughout, senior officers were unfamiliar with conditions on the ground.

The massive build-up of British forces did not escape the attention of the enemy, who had ample time to perfect massive and powerful defences. Often underground, the troops could shelter from the bombardment and emerge unscathed in time to meet the British onslaught.

The High Command – mostly from the cavalry – had great faith in the use of cavalry to exploit a breakthrough once the siege warfare had become a war of movement. This did not happen till late in 1918 and even then, for example, on 8 August, near Horbonnères, on the Somme, a dozen armoured cars achieved more than an entire cavalry brigade. Against prepared positions men and horses simply presented bigger targets, and the incessant machine guns just cut them to ribbons, as happened to the Indian Cavalry Division on 6 July.

The artillery were outgunned in quality and effectiveness. Although British field guns firing shrapnel were technically capable of clearing barbed wire, there had not been enough training and practice and in only one part of the front was the wire successfully cut. Not by coincidence, this was the only part of the advance that was successful.

Despite firing over 1,000,000 shells, 598 German field guns and 246 heavier pieces survived the initial seven-day bombardment and were particularly effective in disposing of those units who had achieved some success.

And, of course, there was the machine gun. The Germans had many more machine guns per unit than the British and had had plenty of time in which to ensure their best siting.

As for the McCraes, what additional problems did they have to contend with? One was the behaviour of 'Inky Bill' (Major General Ingouville-Williams, Officer Commanding 34 Division). Inky Bill was absolutely fearless, with a long string of service and commendations. He was always up at the front, conducting his own reconnaissance patrols, which must have discouraged the normal intelligence channels. Despite what was said above about the ignorance of the top brass, it must be asked whether a subaltern's job was the best outlet for the general in command of ten battalions.

Not unrelated, there was a communications problem which caused chaos. Wilkinson and Alexander differ in detail on this. Basically, communication with the front line was by cable telephone. Once the troops had gone over the top communication was made by runners, so a message asking for more ammunition may have taken two hours to get through. The artillery had their plan for a rolling bombardment which advanced as the infantry took successive objectives. But there was no way progress could be reported and the plan changed – if necessary. So, on occasion, the troops lagged behind, giving the Germans time to emerge from their dugouts and man the machine-guns. Occasionally, the troops got ahead of their timetable and became the recipients of 'friendly fire'.

According to Wilkinson, battalion commanders (like McCrae) and their HQ staff were to advance with their men (losing contact with those viewing the big picture). Alexander states that Brigadier General Gore withdrew all the battalion HQs from the attack. Whatever the truth, the result was a complete disjunction between what was happening in the front line and those who should have been controlling the battle.

One consequence was a shortage of ammunition. Men were killed scavenging for bullets and bandoliers from the dead.

A main objective for the battalion was a ridge defended by 15 lines of defence. Both 15th and 16th Royal Scots were caught in the flank by machine-guns firing from the ruins of the village of La Boiselle.

The two deep Lochnagar mines, whose explosions opened up a crater 100 yards across, left the German trench behind them untouched. Tunnels under the position, which could have eased the movement of reinforcements and supplies, were not made known to the Royal Scots.

On the day, rightly or wrongly, McCrae established his HQ forward and was involved in the fighting:

> The Colonel was a marksman, he took his rifle, and with his servant spotting for him, dropped a Fritz with every shot.

At 10.00am McCrae was placed in command of all forward troops of 34 Division:

> A tall, grey-haired soldier appeared out of a dugout, minus helmet, quite unperturbed by the war and the general mix-up of troops and apparent chaos. He wandered about in a nasty bombardment as if taking a stroll round his garden miles away.

Twenty-one officers and 793 other ranks of the 16th took part in the attack on 1 July. At the end of the day, 12 officers and 624 other ranks were missing from their companies.

On 5 July, the remains of the regiment marched out of the front line and several gallantry awards were approved with immediate effect. Sir George was awarded a DSO and was Mentioned in Dispatches. There were also awards of a DCM, two Military Crosses and four Military Medals. Who knows how many acts of heroism went unrecognized because there was no officer present?

This was not the end of the Sad Story. Reinforcements – five green new subalterns and 400 other ranks from other units – were drafted in on 10 July, diluting the original McCrae mix.

On 30 July they were back in the front line and on 3 August another attack was made with no precise instructions. Inky Bill was dead by now and for his successor, Major-General Nicholson, his first action was a disaster. The butcher's bill for the McCraes was 30 dead and over 100 wounded.

Nicholson – who had not even visited the unit – launched an enquiry 'into the state of the Royal Scots', blaming McCrae. It has been suggested that his crime was that he was too careful of the lives of his men. (It is ridiculous to suppose that a battalion commander should be responsible for the conduct of a battle. Like a private, he carries out the orders of his superior officer. It was 1921 before Nicholson – otherwise a good soldier – accepted his mistake).

Soon, McCrae and his men were to go off in separate directions. On 19 August, Sir George went into hospital. On 14 September he was given command of 101 Brigade. He then returned to the 16th looking very old – he was 55 and had been through hell in recent weeks. It was later discovered that he had been suffering from typhoid. By a stroke of irony in October, he acted as Divisional Commander while Nicholson, his persecutor, went on leave.

He was then informed that 'he was not thought medically fit for further service in France' and left 'quite broken-hearted' on 25 November.

On 9 April 1917 began the next year's 'Big Push' the Battle of Arras. 610 of the 16th took part in the battle, of these 310 were unaccounted for – but at least 60 were dead. After nine days 'relief', the 16th were back in action at the Chemical Works at Roeux. After another botched attack by Nicholson, six officers and 170 men were 'missing'.

At Hargicourt in August the reckoning was two officers and almost 60 men dead, nine officers and at least 130 men wounded.

Every school child has actively role-played the horrors of Passchendaele. On 8 October, the 34th Division – which included McCrae's – were rushed in to carry out a late breakthrough against 'a defensive system of awesome strength'. Again, the losses of the 16th were heavy.

Overall, Haig's Flanders offensive gained only five miles, at a cost of almost 70,000 British and empire soldiers.

Many clever people have suggested that we over-emphasise the first day of the Battle of the Somme, and that we should see it in a much wider context. The Battle of the Somme lasted from 1 July till 18 November, and at the end of it the German pressure on Verdun had been relieved. It is suggested that the Somme was merely the beginning of modern all-arms warfare, when the British caught up with the continental armies. We hear the old canard of the jobsworth being trotted out – 'Lessons were learnt' – but it was two years before there was much sign of that.

There are great debates about numbers, but the British Official History of 1932 recorded that the British suffered 419,654 casualties, the French 194,451 and the Germans 455,332. The battle could 'be viewed as an Allied attritional success' in that the Germans ended the battle exhausted and their losses were more damaging to their force and morale. Put crudely, we could make up half a million – especially when the Americans came in – but the Germans couldn't. One is reminded of first games of chess in which pieces are boringly exchanged between the players until there are not enough pieces left on the board for either player to force a win.

Having knocked Russia out of the war, a million German troops could be transferred to the Western Front, and on 21 March 1918 the Germans attacked 'with clinical precision'. McCrae's had to learn quickly how to defend and retreat without losing all cohesion. Haig issued his famous Special Order: 'Every position must be held to the last man. There must be no retirement.' Jack Alexander, historian of the 16th Royal Scots, reminds us – 'Of course, he was 30 miles *behind* the 'wall' when he wrote it'. (JA's italics).

However, on 25 April, General Erich Ludendorff had to call off the offensive as both his troops and his ammunition were exhausted.

On 16 May, 34 Division (including the 16th Royal Scots) was disbanded for lack of replacements. Most of the battalion were transferred to the 2nd Royal Scots, while the officers and NCOs were sent to train the American Expeditionary Force.

In 1919 McCrae's surviving officers had a 'grand dinner' in the North British Hotel, Edinburgh. But something was missing – the men.

So, on 15 December, the first Reunion Dinner of the 16th Royal Scots was held at the Victoria Hall in Leith Street. Captain Bob Martin was in the chair and gave the boys a song:

> Did ye stand wi' McCrae on the German hill?
> Did ye feel the shrapnel flyin'?
> Did ye close wi' the Hun, comin' in for the kill?
> Did ye see your best friends dyin'?
> Well there's those that will say that they stood wi' McCrae
> And there's those mair content just tae think it.
> Now, we each rise and stand for the Toast to the DEID,
> All those lads never able to drink it.
> McCrae's Battalion!

At the Reunion, a resolution was passed that a 'fitting memorial' be created. Edinburgh Corporation declined to support the proposal – not its last demonstration of ingratitude and indifference. It is as if the Corporation had wished that the battalion had been anonymous as well as eponymous.

So the 16th Royal Scots Association decided to go it alone and Sir George sent out invitations to contribute towards the necessary £1,000.

Raising the money took 14 months, but on Sunday 17 December 1927 the survivors marched from George Street to the High Kirk of St Giles, where, after a service and the handing over of the Regimental Colours, the memorial tablet was unveiled. The service ended with Willie Duguid – who had been with the Gordons on the Heights of Dargai in 1897 and had come through the whole Great War as a stretcher-bearer, carrying Lord knows how many broken bodies back to safety – piping up 'Dark Lochnagar' and a lone bugler sounding the 'Last Post' and 'Reveille'.

By then, the memorial to the Heart of Midlothian fallen had been paid for by the club's supporters and unveiled before a crowd of 40,000.

Jack Alexander contrasts the Hearts monument – its cost and position – with the St Giles plaque, tucked away as if the city was ashamed of it. However, I cannot agree with Alexander on this. The north aisle of St Giles is devoted to memorial plaques to the Royal Scots, Royal Scots Fusiliers, Royal Scots Greys and others. All pretty uniform, dull and interesting to only a few.

But, whether by accident or design, the memorial to the 16th catches all the light there is and closes the view from the west door of the church. PLATE 3A. In rose-coloured limestone, it was designed by Sir Robert Lorimer (who was also responsible for the Scottish National War Memorial in Edinburgh Castle) and carved by Cd'O Pilkington Jackson. It shows an armed St Michael triumphing over a dying Prussian dragon.

The inscription reads:

To the Glory of God
In honoured memory of
Eight hundred officers
Non-commissioned officers
And men
of the 16th (S) Battalion
The Royal Scots (2nd Edin)
who fell in the war
1914–1918

And what of Sir George, whom we last met being sent home from France as a scapegoat? In December 1916, he was promoted to Brigadier-general. He was 'on duty at the War Office' and was to return to France 'in an administrative capacity'. But next month, he left the Army to go back to his old duties at the Local Government Board. Four Prime Ministers, present, former and yet to come – Lloyd George, Asquith, Bonar Law and Churchill – paid tribute and sent their warmest regards.

At home he found his earlier work in ruins, but was appointed to head up the new Scottish Board of Health and implement the 1919 Housing Act, which was, in his view: 'Quite inadequate. Incapable of meeting a grave and dangerous situation.'

Tired of fighting battles with inadequate resources, he left the Board and stood for Parliament as a Liberal. At the second attempt, he was elected for Falkirk and Stirling Burghs. He quickly acquired some influence at a high level, but lost his seat at the General Election of 1922 when the Liberal party went into meltdown and lost 119 seats.

After a series of strokes McCrae died on 14 December 1928. 'You might have thought the King had passed away'. 200 veterans followed the gun carriage, with the coffin, the medals, the sword and the glengarry he had worn instead of a steel helmet at the Scots Redoubt on 1 July 1916. The turn-out was the largest ever seen in Scotland, estimated at 100,000.

Why? As *The Scotsman* said:

> That familiar figure with its buoyant, eager step, the striking face crowned with the gleaming white hair, the instant greeting of a truly friendly spirit, the boyish zest and characteristic gestures. Here was a personality vivid and powerful, and it is not easy to think of him as gone from our midst. But we remember gratefully how much he has given, and still more how much cannot be taken away.

The *Evening News* put it more simply, pointing a moral:

> Sir George was always a trier. He was never discouraged by transient failure. He kept at it and won through. He was kindly and genial. There was nothing of the stern martinet about him. To the working classes he was a real comrade, and to the cause of democracy he was always true.

Anonymous or eponymous? The researcher seeking to photograph McCrae's headstone in the Grange Cemetery is in for a surprise. According to the cemetery records, his grave has no headstone, but lies between A35 (Jessie Sleigh) and A39 (Robert Smith). Poor McCrae! His regiment has been almost painted out of history and even his last resting place is anonymous. McCrae's wife Lizzie (Eliza Cameron Russell) died in 1913, supposedly 15 years to the day before her husband. Her grave also, according to the records, has no headstone, and is next to her husband's.

This is almost unbelievable. McCrae was an important local celebrity and probably quite wealthy. Surely there must be some mistake?

Indeed there has been. Somehow, when the database information was collected in 2004, a fine, but not extravagant, eight-foot Celtic cross was missed. It carries the following inscription:

> In loving memory of
> Eliza Cameron Russell
> Wife of Sir George McCrae
> Died 26th December 1913
>
> Also of
> Sir George McCrae D.S.O.
> Died 27th December 1928.

Around the base are the details of their family.[3]

So, for the researcher on foot, Sir George's last resting place is not anonymous. For the internet browser, however, a totally wrong impression is given.

Alexander's last chapter makes for depressing reading, as it chronicles what happened to McCrae's veterans when they returned to 'the land fit for heroes'. Some survived to turn out again in World War II, and a few did well in their careers. But too many carried the scars – physical and mental – of the awful conflict of which they had been part.

Post-traumatic stress syndrome was not recognised in those days, but, to quote Alexander for the last time:

> 17 suicides have been identified among battalion veterans in the 30 years after 1918; there were probably more.

This has been one of the saddest of stories, not just because of the destruction of a thousand and more lives, but because so many were the result of bad luck or incompetence. Nothing can compensate for this, but Jack Alexander has continued to remind the world of the loyalty and resolution of McCrae and his men.

In 1919 an application was made to the War Office's Battle Exploit Memorials Committee for a memorial at Contalmaison. This was refused, but 85 years later, in 2004, the 'Contalmaison Cairn', constructed by Scottish craftsmen using Scottish materials, was completed. This was the most ambitious battalion memorial to be built on the Western Front since the 1920s:

And has now become something of an international phenomenon, inspiring an annual ceremony of Remembrance and drawing visitors from across the globe. It's a fitting tribute to Sir George and his lads.

In 2006, the McCrae's Battalion Trust was set up, with a splendid website at www.mccraesbattaliontrust.org.uk. In 2011, the story of McCrae's became the principal tableau of the famous 'Pozières Son et Lumière' spectacle. On 27 November 2014, at a big celebratory meeting in the Usher Hall, the space around the Hall was renamed 'McCrae's Place', exactly 100 years since his great recruiting meeting there. The latest news is that Raith Rovers, the Kirkcaldy football team, 'have a stunning new commemorative McCrae's away strip'.

All is not lost – and all done by local enterprise, without Mr Cameron's £60 million.

Notes

1   Jack Alexander calls this the 'Lancastrian School'. In fact, it was a Heriot Trust school run on the Lancastrian system. As well as the parent institution, George Heriot's Hospital, the Trust operated several schools in poorer parts of the city. After the Education Act of 1872, the best nine of these were purchased or rented by the Edinburgh School Board.

   The Hospital ceased to be residential, becoming a day school – George Heriot's School. When the 16th was raised, their first quarters were in Heriot's Examination Hall and Art Department, connected by a bridge to a brewery outside the school wall.

   The 'Heriot's men', as these 'founder members' were called, enjoyed a special cachet within the battalion as, sadly, time went by and their numbers diminished.

2   Peter Ross rose to be Captain Ross. On 1 July he was the last remaining officer in A Company. To quote Alexander:

   He gathered the remnants of his command in order to rush a second machine gun. The gunner shot him in the stomach, almost cutting him in two... Ross, meanwhile, was still alive and in unimaginable pain. He begged someone to finish him off. In the end, it came down to an order. Two of his own men reluctantly obliged. One of the witnesses was to kill himself twenty years later.

3   On all four sides of the base are recorded the names of their children and families, among them:

Also their son
Captain George McCrae
The Royal Scots
Died in action at Gallipoli 28th June 1915
Aged 31 years

(This was the botched attack masterminded by 'Hunter-Bunter' a
week after disembarkation and mentioned in Chapter 2)

Also their daughter
Senior Commander Fiona McCrae MBE 1948
Aged 43 years.
(Died in Millbank Military Hospital, London)

Also their son
Major William Russell McCrae MC
Died 24th January 1950
Aged 64 years

PLATE 1A

A Black Watch Highlander in full dress uniform. Norah Geddes used to watch the soldiers pass from her window.

Black Watch Boer War Memorial, The Mound, Edinburgh

PLATE 1B

Bronze plinth depicting a battle charge of Highlanders.

Black Watch Boer War Memorial The Mound, Edinburgh

PLATE 2A

Mass grave of the Quintinshill disaster victims. These soldiers lost their lives in the terrible train crash, in 1915.

Memorial and Roll of Honour, Rosebank Cemetery, Edinburgh.

PLATE 2B

This is the memorial to those from the Heart of Midlothian Football Club who fell in the Great War, many from 'McCrae's Battalion'

Hearts War Memorial, Haymarket, Edinburgh.

PLATE 3A

Memorial to 16th Battalion The Royal Scots, St Giles, Edinburgh. The inscription reads:

'To the Glory of God
In honoured memory of
Eight hundred officers
Non-commissioned officers
And men
of the 16th (S) Battalion
The Royal Scots (2nd Edin)
who fell in the war
1914–1918'

PLATE 3B

The military hospital, in Edinburgh, for officers suffering from shell shock, where Siegfried Sassoon and Wilfred Owen resided.

Slateford Military Hospital at Craiglockhart Cover of Folio Society's edition of *Sherston's Progress*

PLATE 4A

Siegfried Sassoon believed that golf had value as therapy and spent many hours on this course.

Mortonhall Golf Club, Braid Hills, Edinburgh

PLATE 4B

The pharmacy and the post office are as close to a core as one could find in Craiglockhart.

'Hillside' by Lara Greene.

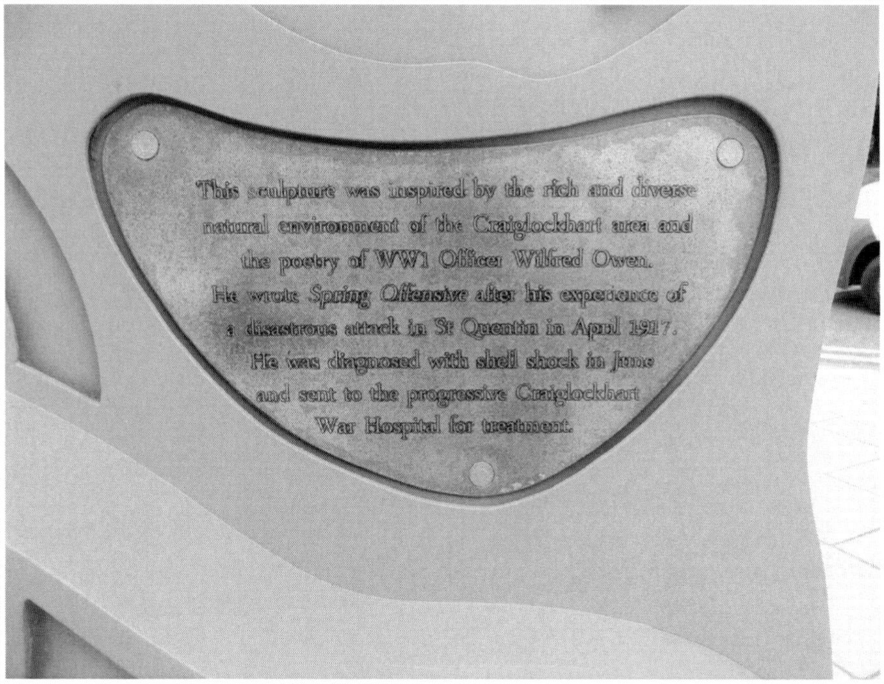

PLATE 5A

The inscription reads:

'This sculpture was inspired by the rich and diverse natural environment of the Craiglockhart area and the poetry of World War I officer Wilfred Owen.

He wrote 'Spring Offensive' after his experience of a disastrous attack in St Quentin in April 1917. He was diagnosed with shell shock in June and sent to the progressive Craiglockhart War Hospital for treatment.'

'Hillside' by Lara Greene.

PLATE 5B

An unusually extravagant dedication to the fallen.
Glenelg War Memorial, Highland

PLATE 6A
Memorial to two wars,
Bracadale, Skye.
The simple homage of an
island community.

PLATE 6B
Commonwealth War Graves
Commission graves, Comely
Bank Cemetery, Edinburgh.
All in good order and with
military discipline.

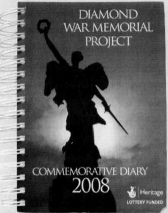

PLATE 7A

Above:

'Their Name Liveth'?

War graves in a forgotten corner of Newington Cemetery, Edinburgh

PLATE 7B

Left:

The Commemorative Diary recorded the names, rank and numbers of those who were killed on that day.

Diamond War Memorial Project, 2008, Ulster

PLATE 7C

Below:

A small museum of items (dating from the Crimea) contributed by former residents of Somme Park.

The Museum, Somme Park, Londonderry

PLATE 8A

Inside this memorial are recorded the names of the Scots who died in the two world wars, and in more recent conflicts. Included are the names of 206,285 individuals who died in the Great War

Scottish National War Memorial, Edinburgh Castle

PLATE 8B

This commemorates the Battle of Jutland, the only major naval battle of the Great War. It remains intentionally unfinished, representing the many lives cut short by warfare.

War Memorial, Stonehaven, Aberdeenshire

CHAPTER 6

The War Poets in the Eye of the Storm

ONE OF THE CONCERNS of an old gentleman like myself is the constant corruption and debasement of our language. Just as Gresham's Law tells us that bad money drives out good, stupid or pretentious people make accurate use of language almost impossible. 'Disinterested' is a good word which meant that one did not, for example, aim to profit from one's advice. When many people began to use it as a synonym for 'uninterested', it became ambiguous and lost its value.

A fault in the natural world is a break in the Earth's crust, with a displacement of the rock on either, or both, sides. For example, the Central Lowlands of Scotland lie between the Highland Boundary Fault (running from Helensburgh to Stonehaven) and the Southern Uplands Boundary Fault (from Girvan to Dunbar). When a Prime Minister starts talking about the 'fault-lines in the economy' as something terrible to be eradicated he is talking nonsense. The Highland Boundary Fault is neither good nor bad, it is just a fact to be lived with. But now we have fault-lines everywhere.

One of my pet hates is the misuse of 'the eye of the storm', which even weather forecasters seem to think is the worst part. In our mid-latitudes, much of our rain comes from depressions originating in the mid-Atlantic and moving, fairly slowly, north-eastwards. The typical depression comes with south-westerly winds and steady rain. As it moves on – and one is lucky – the rain stops and the wind drops. Then the wind gets up again, it backs to become north-westerly and the weather becomes showery, often with brilliant bright intervals.

In the tropics, our comparatively gentle depressions can become very intense and fast-moving, particularly in late summer. As hurricanes and typhoons they can be terribly destructive, both as winds and via the storm surges the winds force on to the land. Again there is a pattern of ferocious winds, in the Northern Hemisphere usually from the south-west, then a quiet spell, when the local inhabitants come out and begin to assess the damage, and those at sea try to restore the rigging that has been swept away. This is the eye of the storm. After this brief respite, the barometer rises again, the wind backs to the north-west and the furious onslaught of the 'returning air' commences – often more destructive than the first phase.

For the best-known War Poets, Siegfried Sassoon and Wilfred Owen, Slateford Military Hospital, in Edinburgh, was the 'eye of the storm' between the horrors of one phase of the war and the next.

Like Rome, Edinburgh is often said to be situated on seven hills. In the case of Edinburgh, the Castle Rock, Calton Hill and Arthur's Seat are very central; Corstorphine Hill lies over to the north-west, while the Braid Hills and the two Craiglockhart Hills, Easter and Wester lie south of the city's core. The pleasant slopes running down to the Jordan Burn from these latter hills acquired institutions seeking peace and quiet and, in the late 19th century, the reassuring suburbs of Morningside and Craiglockhart spread up and around the hills.

The Edinburgh Asylum (which was to evolve into the Royal Edinburgh Hospital) opened in Morningside in 1813. Craighouse (private) Asylum opened on Easter Craiglockhart Hill in 1894. Also on Easter Craiglockhart Hill was Morningside Hydropathic, which closed in 1882; the building then becoming Morningside College for Boys, and, in turn, became the temporary home of the Royal Edinburgh Hospital for Sick Children for five years.

The Craiglockhart estate belonged to the remarkable Monros. Dr Alexander Monro was the first Professor of Anatomy at Edinburgh, and for 128 years, three generations of Monros made Edinburgh a worldwide name in the field of medicine. On the death of Dr Alexander Monro (*tertius*) the estate passed to trustees who broke it up. On the eastern slopes of Wester Craiglockhart Hill, the New City Poorhouse was opened in 1870, and nearby – at a suitable distance from the city – the new Edinburgh City Fever Hospital was opened in 1903.

Just below the steep western slopes of Wester Craiglockhart Hill, near but quite separate from this complex of medical institutions, was established, in 1880, Craiglockhart Hydropathic. Edinburgh architects Peddie and Kinnear produced a 'giant Italian villa', 'majestic, almost palatial'. Imposing it certainly was – and still is – but the interior tended to be on the sombre side. According to Groome's *Ordnance Gazetteer of Scotland* of 1882:

The rich and poor of the city (the wealthy residents of the luxurious hydropathic and the paupers in nearby Craiglockhart Poorhouse) could now reside on the same hill.

And what a hill it was! Wooded, with walks and romantic cliffs, wonderful views over the city and over half of south-east Scotland, a sporting golf course between the hills, a curling pond and Craiglockhart Pond for boating and skating in the winter.

The early days of the hydro were troubled, but after purchase at a knock-down price by the lessee of Dunblane Hydro, it became more viable. Nevertheless, the management must have been relieved when the hydro was requisitioned as a military hospital for officers suffering from neurasthenia (shell-shock). PLATE 3B.

Into this privileged situation, on 25 June 1917, came one Wilfred Owen:

His nerves finally shattered by a fall into a cellar in the trenches and twelve days in 'no-man's land'.

A month later, he was joined by Siegfried Sassoon. Owen was almost unknown to the staff at Craiglockhart, while Sassoon was already notorious.

The name 'Sassoon' was certainly one to play with. The Sassoons originated in Baghdad before moving to Bombay and Shanghai, becoming immensely rich from cotton and opium in the process. In late Victorian Britain, David Sassoon of Bombay (1793–1864) led the family into the highest echelon of society. Reuben Sassoon (1835–1905) became the unofficial turf accountant of Edward, Prince of Wales. In Hamilton Place, where:

Cheek by jowl with older examples of newish money, Lady Londonderry and Lord Northbrook, mining and banking, respectively – lived two of the newest *nouveaux riches*: Sir Richard Garton, a millionaire three times over from the profits of brewing sugar; and Marcus Samuel, co-founder of the mighty Shell petroleum company. Here also lived Meyer Elias Sassoon [grandson of David] and two men whose houses summed up the millionaire style to perfection... Leopold Albu, a German-South African mining financier... and Leopold de Rothschild, a leading member of the Prince of Wales's racing set.

By 1903, the King (Edward VII, freed from his mother's apron strings at last) was 'weekending at Brighton in the company of... the Sassoons'. By now the Sassoons had estates in Sussex and Kent, and the obligatory shooting box in Scotland. Barney Barnato, a Jewish diamond millionaire, had built for himself a huge, ugly, house at 25 Park Lane. When he was drowned at sea in mysterious circumstances, Sir Edward Albert Sassoon (1856–1912) bought the house and turned it 'into a plutocrat's dream'.

It is likely that, just before 1914,

> Over one-fifth of all non-landed millionaires were Jews, although the Jewish population of London was no more than 3 per cent of the total, and the Jewish proportion of the British population as a whole was only 0.3 per cent. London's leading Jews emerged as lords paramount of smart Society.

Not everyone was happy with this state of affairs. Although money could buy its way almost anywhere, even at the highest level there was resistance and condescension. In 1864, two Rothschilds were blackballed in a single night at Brooks's, the London club 'which was still a bastion of the great Whig motherhood'. Popular novelists featured international conspiracies and villainous Jews. Middle-class Jews in north-west London had to set up their own golf club because no other would accept them.

Siegfried Sassoon (1886–1967) was the second son of Alfred Ezra Sassoon (1861–1895) who married – outside the faith – Theresa Thornycroft. As a result Alfred was disinherited. Siegfried's parents separated when he was four years old, and his father died when he was nine. Siegfried was fortunate in having enough of a fortune to live modestly without ever having to work for a living. When he was not at prep school, Marlborough and Cambridge (where he spent two years studying history, without graduating) he was brought up by his aunt Rachel Beer, whose generous legacy many years later enabled him to buy an estate in Wiltshire. Not the most stable of childhoods. In the years running up to the Great War, Sassoon was on the fringes of literary society, but his abiding interest was fox-hunting, followed a long way behind by cricket.

We know a great deal about Sassoon's inner life because he wrote so well about it. In 1928, after a decade or so of poetry, was published *Memoirs of a Fox-Hunting Man*, which won the 1928 James Tait Black Award for fiction. Yes, fiction. We must remember this when we look on it as a historical source. In 1930, *Memoirs of an Infantry Officer* followed, then *Sherston's Progress* in 1936. The three books were published together in 1937 as *The Complete Memoirs of George Sherston*. George Sherston is, of course, a thinly disguised Sassoon and his trilogy is a beautifully written account of how he came to be in Craiglockhart, what it was like to be there and what happened after.

It may be my Presbyterian Scottish background, but I find the pre-war Sassoon thoroughly disagreeable – but horribly fascinating. One is reminded of Oscar Wilde's description of fox-hunting, that the English country gentleman galloping after a fox was 'the unspeakable in full pursuit of the uneatable'. The last two chapters of *Memoirs of a Fox-Hunting Man* take us into the Great War. Sassoon enlisted as a trooper in the Sussex Yeomanry (Territorial Army cavalry) two days before the declaration of war and volunteered for service abroad. After two months, he 'began to be definitely bored with Yeomanry life'. A bad fall resulted in a very badly broken arm and it was May 1915 before he was able to take up his duties as a Second Lieutenant in what he called the Royal Flintshire Fusiliers (actually the 3rd Battalion (Special Reserve) Royal Welsh Fusiliers).

The 'poor bloody infantry' must have been rather a come-down after the cavalry, (and Sassoon has something to say about his fellow-officers, most of them) but Sassoon did his best at the training depot, and was sent out in September to join the First Battalion near Béthune, where:

> My platoon accepted me apathetically. It was a diminished and exhausted little platoon, and its mind was occupied with anticipations of 'Divisional Rest'.

After some miserable days in the front line, Sassoon showed that he could learn from others. Julian Durley was

> A shy, stolid-faced platoon commander who had been a clerk in Somerset House. He took the men's discomforts very much to heart. Simple and unassertive, he liked sound literature and had a sort of metropolitan turn of humour. His jokes, when things were going badly, reminded me of a facetious bus conductor on a wet winter day. Durley was an inspiration towards selfless patience. He was an ideal platoon officer, and an example which I tried to imitate from that night onward. I need hardly say that he had never hunted. He could swim like a fish, but no social status was attached to that.

In the *Memoirs of an Infantry Officer* Sassoon takes us into the busy life of the trenches, broken only by an interlude at the Fourth Army School, where the lectures

Failed to convince me of their affinity with our long days and nights in the Front Line.

These were delivered by instructors 'all in favour of Open Warfare', which they had learnt all about in peace time.

It would be easy to dismiss Sassoon as a simple snob, as when he says something like:

The deportment of a 'temporary gentleman' enjoying his last decent dinner was apt to be more suitable to a dug-out than a military club.

Or says he was 'talking to a Northumberland Fusiliers officer who drops his aitches'. Sassoon

Always found that it was a distinct asset, when in close contact with officers of the Regular Army, to be able to converse convincingly about hunting. It gave one an almost unfair advantage in some ways.

One who writes about 'English armies' does not endear himself to one from the nation which over-contributed so much to the eventual victory, but while he may be patronising towards some of the other ranks, he becomes increasingly sympathetic towards their plight.

To be fair to Sassoon, he was an outsider who felt 'it was a luxury to be alone' and had doubts about his competence. He felt that 'if only I could get a Military Cross, I should feel comparatively safe and confident' and pushed himself into the exciting and dangerous life of night patrols and trench raids.

One such trench raid went horribly wrong; the raiders were caught out in the open in a tangle of uncut wire and beat a hasty retreat – most of them. Sassoon – who had not been in the raiding party, tidied up the mess in no-mans-land and brought in the wounded:

I prided myself on having pulled off something rather heroic; but when all was said and done it was only the sort of thing which people often did during a fire or a railway accident.

But it earned him his MC.

Around 5 July, Sassoon found himself in the newly captured Quadrangle Trench, with everyone else around lackadaisical and exhausted. Sassoon and Lance-Corporal Kendle pushed forward until Kendle was shot by a sniper, whereupon – like a Hollywood hero – Sassoon slung a bag of bombs over his shoulder and set off at the double 'to settle that sniper'. He came to a trench with 50 or 60 Germans in it, who ran away, leaving all their equipment behind. In the newly captured sniping post, he meditated for a few minutes 'somewhat like a boy who has caught a fish too big to carry home', then took a deep breath 'and ran headlong back by the way I'd come'.

On his return to Battalion HQ, his Colonel gave him hell. Why hadn't he come back – as ordered – with the company bombers? Why hadn't he consolidated Wood Trench? Why the hell hadn't he sent back a message to let him know that it had been occupied? The Corps Artillery bombardment had been held up for three hours because he (Colonel Kinjack) could not report that 'Sassoon's patrol' had returned to Quadrangle Trench.

That evening was another turning point. Sassoon's battalion marched out into reserve and were relieved by 'a jostling company of exclamatory Welshmen' – 'a panicky rabble', 'mostly undersized', 'bewildered', 'half-trained civilians'. Sassoon 'had a sense of their victimisation'.

> Visualising that forlorn crowd of khaki figures… I saw then, for the first time, how blindly war destroys its victims… Two days later the Welsh Division, of which they were a unit, was involved in massacre and confusion.

Part Five is entitled 'Escape'. Sassoon had contracted enteritis and was evacuated to No 2 Red Cross Hospital. A 'genial doctor', carrying *The Times,* examined him:

> My name caused him to consult *The Times.* 'Is this you?' he asked. Sure enough my name was there, in a list of Military Crosses which chanced to have appeared that day. The doctor patted me on the shoulder and informed me that I should be going across to England next day. Good luck had 'wangled me home'… I was involved in one of the lesser miracles of the Great War.

For the record, Sassoon was awarded the Military Cross on 27 July 1916. The citation read:

> 2nd Lt Siegfried Lorraine (sic) Sassoon, 3rd (attd 1st) R W Fus.
>
> For conspicuous gallantry during a raid on the enemy's trenches. He remained for 1 1/2 hours under rifle and bomb fire collecting and bringing in our wounded. Owing to his courage and determination all the killed and wounded were brought in.

In hospital in Oxford, and on two subsequent spells on sick leave, Sassoon had plenty of time to reflect on the disparity between his war and the war as reported at home, to hear occasionally the sound of gunfire drifting across the Channel and to read of the calamities being suffered by his regiment.

For the third winter of the War, 'cured' and restored, he was sent to the Regimental Depot near Liverpool.

> The raw material to be trained was growing steadily worse. Most of those who came in now had joined the Army unwillingly, and there was no reason why they should find military service tolerable... What in earlier days had been drafts of volunteers were droves of victims. I was just beginning to be aware of this.

Then it was the 5th Infantry Base Depot at Rouen (the infamous 'Bull Ring') where the notice board carried the names of those going up to the Line next day, and of three privates shot for cowardice. For the first time, Sassoon lets himself go on the contrast between the Front Line and the Base. He was posted to the 2nd Battalion of the Flintshires, fought through the Battle of Arras and ended up in a London hospital with 'a neat hole' through him, just missing his jugular vein and spine. It was now, in a few hospitals and as a guest of 'Lady Asterix' that he 'began to think' and really became critical and inquiring about the War.

Using his name and military record he lunched with the editor of the *Unconservative Weekly* at his club and allowed himself to be drawn into an Anti-War circle. He prepared what he himself described

> As an act of wilful defiance of military authority, because I believe the war is being deliberately prolonged.

He sent this to his Commanding Officer when he was summoned back to the Depot, saying that he would not report for duty until something was done about the situation. The statement included the following, which some regarded as treasonable:

> I believe that the war upon which I entered as a war of defence and liberation has now become a war of aggression and conquest.

It made its way into the press and was read out by a sympathetic MP in the House of Commons, causing the military authorities great embarrassment. However, the Army has great experience in handling difficult subordinates. Sassoon went up before a Medical Board, who noticed his military experience and proven gallantry, and decided that he must be suffering from shell-shock. They couldn't do better than send him to Slateford War Hospital. And, unescorted, off he went to Slateford, rather like those Victorian wives whose husbands had tired of them and had them certified and locked up in a lunatic asylum.

Wilfred Owen's journey to Slateford could hardly have been more different. Born in 1893, he was born near Oswestry, in Shropshire. His father was a stationmaster, with the result that young Owen was moved around in his formative years, from Oswestry to Birkenhead, to Shrewsbury, back to Birkenhead, then back again to Shrewsbury, back to Birkenhead again, and back, yet again, to Shrewsbury in 1907.

Young Owen was educated at the Birkenhead Institute and at Shrewsbury Technical School. In 1909, he became a pupil-teacher at the Wyle Cop School in Shrewsbury. In 1911, he passed the matriculation examination for the University of London. However, the only way he could have attended London would have been through a scholarship – and for this first-class honours would have had to be attained.

Owen's mother was a strong Anglican, very influential, and one of his early influences was the Bible. Owen became a lay assistant to the Vicar of Dunsden, near Reading, attending classes in botany and Old English at University College, Reading. During his time at Dunsden he lost his faith, disillusioned by Church ceremonial and the failure to provide aid for those in need.

From 1913, he worked as a private tutor teaching English and French in the Berlitz School of Languages in Bordeaux, and later with a family. At the outbreak of war, unlike a John Buchan hero, he did not rush home to enlist. He considered joining the French army, but eventually returned to England where, in October 1915, he enlisted in the Artists' Rifles Officers' Training Corps (Sassoon would have been in the OTC when at Marlborough, acquiring the necessary qualifications for a commission).

In June 1916, he was commissioned as a Second Lieutenant into the Manchester Regiment. Initially, he showed himself as much of a snob as Sassoon, despising those under his command as 'expressionless lumps'. Like Sassoon, he had his ups and downs – literally. He fell into a shell hole and suffered concussion. He was blown high into the air by a trench mortar. He spent several days lying out on an embankment in a wood amongst what may have been the remains of a fellow-officer. On 2 May

1917 his Commanding Officer decided he was unwell and he was evacuated to No 13 CSS with shell shock. On 16 June, he was transferred to Netley Hospital in Hampshire, and on 25 June he was sent to Slateford War Hospital for treatment.

This True Story of the War Poets is being structured through *The Complete Memoirs of George Sherston* and Part One of *Sherston's Progress* is 'Rivers'. This is not a disquisition on the flowing, meandering thread of life or an interpretation of Freudian dreams, but the name of Sassoon's psychiatrist at Slateford, a Captain in the RAMC – and an expert on the interpretation of dreams, Freudian or not. Three evenings a week, Sassoon 'went along to Rivers' room to give 'his "anti-war complex" an airing'. A relationship built up, in which Sassoon's 'futile demons' fled him. Rivers':

> Presence was a refutation of wrong-headedness. I knew then that I had been very lonely while I was at the War; I knew that I had a lot to learn, and that he was the only man who could help me.

For Sassoon, life at Slateford was indeed the 'eye of the storm' –for some of which he was himself responsible. A tram from Slateford village, or a Caledonian train from Slateford Station (for which the timetable was published in *The Hydra* – of which more later), took him to Princes Street or the Caledonian Hotel and the delights of café life. (The unknown author of *The Confessions of a Subaltern* in *The Hydra* wrote: 'I have only to go down Princes Street twice and my pay has vanished.') Sassoon had long conversations with his fellow-patients and the occasional visit by 'Stop-the-War' campaigners – although these dried up pretty soon. He lunched with the Astronomer Royal for Scotland. He sent for his golf clubs and set about demonstrating the value of golf as therapy:

> I must admit, though, that I wasn't worrying much about the War when I'd just hit a perfect tee-shot up the charming vista which was the fairway to the first green at Mortonhall. PLATE 4A

In that fourth October of the war he claimed to be a better golfer than he had ever been before – or was ever to be after. 'Most of my days have been spent in slogging golf-balls on the hills above Edinburgh.' His daily match with a chattering Royal Army Medical Corps man was 'an escape from the truly awful atmosphere of this place of wash-outs and shattered heroes'. (There was a weekly golf match between the neighbouring

Merchants of Edinburgh club and the Craiglockhart inmates, but Sassoon does not seem to have taken part in these, preferring to go his own way.) Other activities he might have taken part in – but probably did not – were the weekly regattas of the Model Yacht Club on Craiglockhart Pond and the visit of the Scottish Billiards Champion, which attracted an attendance of 200.

By day, Craiglockhart had

> The melancholy atmosphere of a decayed hydro, redeemed only by its healthy situation and pleasant view of the Pentland Hills. By daylight the doctors dealt successfully with these disadvantages… but by night they lost control and the hospital became sepulchral and oppressive with saturations of war experience.

Sassoon paints a horrific picture of the sufferings of the genuinely shell-shocked, alone with their memories in the dark, and voices his rage at those, sanctioned and glorified by the Churches, who sent them out to maim and slaughter their fellow-men:

> In the name of civilisation these soldiers had been martyred, and it remained for civilisation to prove that their martyrdom wasn't a dirty swindle.

'Shell Shock!' the Frontispiece, is one inmate's interpretation of the plight of the shell-shocked, which appeared in *The Hydra*. Sassoon's sonnet, *Dreamers*, also appeared in *The Hydra*. A gentler picture, it still stirs the emotions.

Dreamers

Soldiers are citizens of death's grey land,
Drawing no dividend from earth's tomorrows.
In the great hour of destiny they stand,
Each with his feuds, and jealousies, and sorrows.
Soldiers are sworn to action; they must win
Some flaming, fatal climax with their lives.
Soldiers are dreamers; when the guns begin
They think of firelit homes, clean beds, and wives.

I see them in foul dug-outs, gnawed by rats,
And in the ruined trenches, lashed with rain,
Dreaming of things they did with balls and bats,

And mocked by hopeless longing to regain
Bank-holidays, and picture-shows, and spats,
And going to the office in the train.

An important feature of *The Complete Memoirs of George Sherston* is the large number of detailed pen-portraits of those around him, usually pseudonymous. For us, looking back, it seems strange that Wilfred Owen does not appear to feature, even in disguise, in *Sherston's Progress*.

Although Owen arrived at Slateford a month before Sassoon, the latter was senior in almost every respect. He was older and had had longer service – Owen, after all, was just one of the despised 'temporary gentlemen'. Sassoon was of the upper crust, had had the appropriate education, and probably confirmed it every time he opened his mouth.

He came to Slateford with a reputation for foolhardy bravery – and with a medal to prove it. And he was in Slateford for having made himself conspicuous in criticizing the establishment.

It was probably the fact that Sassoon was already an established writer that drew them together. Sassoon wrote to Robert Graves:

Little Owen... and made a very good impression... I am sure he will be
a very good poet some day, and he is a very loveable creature.

There is plenty of evidence to show that the two poets became very close. Sassoon encouraged Owen and showed him many of 'the tricks of the trade' without curbing his originality, while Owen simply worshipped Sassoon. (Sassoon does not seem to have been jealous that Owen developed into the better poet. After the War he was influential in Owen's promotion.)

Owen's experience at Slateford differed from Sassoon's. Rivers was a psychoanalyst, Dr Arthur Brock believed in Ergotherapy – the healing power of Work. As a medical student at Edinburgh, Brock had been taught 'Botany' by Patrick Geddes and became a dedicated follower, swallowing whole Geddes's triad of Work, Place, Folk, as a model for the analysis of society.

'Work' for officers could not be bricklaying or gardening, although Major Bryce of the Field Club called for – and got – volunteers to help with the harvest at three local farms. Instead, 'work' for officers was carrying out local surveys, Geddes-style, involving the local people. Dr Brock also drove the Field Club, in which 'Weekly excursions are made to the Edinburgh region, which is being systematically surveyed'.

Owen certainly went out with the Field Club. The Field Club also had lectures, which Owen attended. Most were safe and predictable, but one was very strange. Captain Hyland on 6 August 1917 gave 'an attractive paper' on 'Geology in Flanders', illustrated by blackboard sketches. 'The lecturer recounted his valuable experiences over the earth's crust in that part'. When one considers that perhaps half of his audience might have been blown up as a result of German mining operations, and some of them may have gone on to drown in the mud of Passchendaele in a couple of months' time, one wonders at the choice of subject. From the report, someone like myself cannot tell whether the speaker was serious or ironic. Or was this some kind of shock therapy to force the shell-shocked to face their fears?

Another aspect of Work was for the officers to produce an in-house magazine – *The Hydra*. (Word-play – they were in 'The Hydro'. Also, the hydra was a many-headed monster. When one head was cut off, it was replaced by two. Exactly like many of the dreams the inmates suffered.) Major (Dr) Brock wrote about 'Memories Pedagogic'. Owen edited the magazine and was a major contributor. He was sent down to Geddes's Outlook Tower to research an article and talked to 'the staff'. One of the saddest facts about Owen is that the only poems of his he saw in print (bar one) were those published in *The Hydra*.

It is worthwhile to break off to look briefly at Brock's post-war career, as it continued to link up with Geddes's work in Edinburgh. He set up in private practice in 1919, 'practically confining myself to neurasthenic cases and such, generally as need 're-educative' treatment'. He worked also at Geddes's Outlook Tower, gradually moving into a position of medical humanism. In 1925, he set up a 'convalescent home for nervous patients' at Garth Hill, North Queensferry, which he called his 'little Ferry Hills Outlook Tower', and in 1932 founded the North Queensferry Development Association to do Geddesian things in the local community. By now, he was out of the mainstream of psychology and sociology but translated the works of Galen, the Roman physician and wrote extensively on medical/psychological/sociological issues and local history. He died in 1947. A friend said of him a few days before he died:

> Tears came to his eyes for the sorrows of his fellows blundering, as it seemed to him, from one tragic folly to another. He longed to be active again to continue the fight against evil on earth, and almost his last word

as we parted was of a plan to make a new approach to the desire of his mind and heart – the revival of true communities in the land he loved.

In 1911, the Edinburgh School Board had opened a new school for technical and commercial education for 1,200 in the working-class area of Gorgie-Dalry. It shared the name Tynecastle with the football ground of Heart of Midlothian – whose players figured so prominently as leading recruitment for McRae's Battalion. Owen must have known this, and of the exploits of the battalion, when he was sent down to Tynecastle where he taught for three weeks. He is also supposed to have taken a group of boys to Swanston, where the young Robert Louis Stevenson spent his summers and drew some of his inspiration.

Understandably, Owen-centric commentators have seized on this as evidence of Owen's initiative and his common touch. In fact, Craiglockhart had a Boys' Training Club, of which *The Hydra* says:

> At Tynecastle School, Gorgie, the following classes have been held weekly:
> – Map-reading, 4 classes: Signalling, 2 classes: Physical Drill, 3 classes:
> English Literature, 1 class: First Aid, 1 class. According to the headmaster, these classes are a great success, and he is very keen that they should be continued... Mr Owen took a very successful class in English Literature, and on his departure Mr Bayley has been kindly taking on the work.

Owen's other extra-mural activities included a course in German at the Berlitz School in Edinburgh and regular visits to the Public Baths.

Between 1916 and 1919, 1,801 officers were treated at Craiglockhart. Of these, we are told that 735 were discharged as medically unfit. 167 were given home service of light duties. 141 were given specialist medical treatment in other hospitals and 758 were returned to active service. (So nobody died?) Yet on 30 July, Sassoon wrote to his aunt:

> A few are genuine cases of shell-shock etc. One committed suicide three weeks ago. The bad ones are sent to another place.

Among those restored to the military life were Sassoon and Owen, who must have been considered 'cured' by their time at the military hospital. For Sassoon, it was clear that his protest had been side-lined and that he might have to spend the rest of the war in 'Dottyville' (Sassoon's coinage) – where some of his fellow-officers considered his stand against the war to be a clever 'wangle' to get away from the action. At a medical board on 26 November, Rivers was able to say that Sassoon was 'not suffering from any form of psycho-neurosis' and he was discharged and passed for General Service. As Sassoon wrote: 'No obstacles would be put in the way of my going back to the sausage machine.'

So it was back to the Regimental depot near Liverpool, and Limerick, where he got in some therapeutic hunting. Then there was a mammoth train and ferry journey to France, on to Italy and over to Alexandria. Allenby had cleared out southern Palestine from the Turks and Sassoon spent two months in and around Jerusalem before being summoned back – along with the rest of the Division who had been out there since Gallipoli in 1915 – to the Western Front where the Germans had broken through in the spring. He did not think much of most of his new colleagues:

> O, the coarse stupidity of some of the others. Minds like the front page of the *Daily Mirror*... Suffocating boredom of the forced intimacy of living with them. They see nothing clearly. Minds clogged with mental deadness... The Colonel is odiously vulgar and snobbish; a very bad type of British nobleman.

On 8 June 1918, Sassoon – a full Lieutenant at last – was back in the front line. In the latter half of June, an influenza epidemic upset all the calculations of the High Command and 'more than half the men in our brigade were too ill to leave their billets'. Back in the front line, Sassoon specialised in 'conducted tours' of no man's land as training for the new recruits. On 13 July, after some 'tremendous fun', as Sassoon recorded:

> With my tin hat in my hand I stood up and turned for a moment to look back at the German line.

Moments later, he was shot in the head by what the Americans have taught us to call 'friendly fire', and on 20 July he was back in London, in hospital. There, by now a captain, he was to see out the war in a turmoil of self-doubt.

> I saw myself as one who had achieved nothing except an idiotic anti-climax, and my mind worked itself into a tantrum of self-disparagement. Why hadn't I stayed in France where I could at least escape from the War by being in it? Out there I had never despised my existence as I did now.

Owen's case was less complicated than Sassoon's, and in November 1917 he was adjudged as being fit for light regimental duties at home and discharged from Craiglockhart. The next eight months were productive, as far as his poetry went, being spent in Scarborough and Ripon. Although his poetry terrifyingly portrays the horror and futility of the struggle, Owen does not seem to have been afraid of the real thing. At the end of August 1918 he returned to the front line and, perhaps modelling himself on his hero, Sassoon, threw himself more vigorously than ever into the conduct of hostilities.

In October Owen won his long-sought-after Military Cross:

> For conspicuous gallantry and devotion to duty in the attack on the Fonsomme Line on October 1st/2nd, 1918. On the company commander becoming a casualty, he assumed command and showed fine leadership and resisted a heavy counter-attack. He personally manipulated a captured enemy machine gun from an isolated position and inflicted considerable losses on the enemy. Throughout he behaved most gallantly.

In a reflective mood, Sassoon was to write:

> Nobody knew how much a decoration was worth except the man who received it. Outwardly the distribution of them became more and more fortuitous as the War went on; and no one knew it better than the infantry, who rightly insisted that medal-ribbons earned at the Base ought to be a different colour.

An interesting comment, coming from one who threw his medal ribbon – but not the medal – into the Mersey in a demonstration of some kind and was disappointed that it did not sink but floated accusingly on the surface. Written years after the War, do we detect a whiff of jealousy of the younger, but better, poet?

By now, the Germans were in full retreat and it was clear that the war must end soon. Owen was 'sufficiently rewarded by surges of adrenalin and a sense of heart-warming camaraderie'. On 4 November his unit, the 2nd Manchesters, was involved in an unnecessary action to cross the heavily-defended Sambre and Oise Canal. Whoever masterminded the British attack had clearly learned nothing from four years of war, nor from the great Duke of Wellington a century earlier – 'Press on till you are stopped, then go round'. The British had to assemble a bridge to cross the 70-foot canal before they could engage the enemy:

> Group after group of soldiers went forward and were killed or wounded. Wilfred Owen, standing at the water's edge, was encouraging his men when he was hit and killed.

There is always a special sadness for those killed in the dying phases of a war, when their deaths are doubly irrelevant. The day after his death, Owen was promoted to Lieutenant. In a final indignity:

> Seven days later the war was over. Church bells rang throughout the country. As they were ringing in Shrewsbury, Susan and Tom Owen received the telegram announcing their son's death.

The award of his MC was not gazetted until 15 February 1919 and the citation quoted above did not follow until 20 July 1919. No doubt there was a lot of tidying up to be done after the 11th hour of the 11th day of the 11th month, and anyway, the chap would never know – he was dead, after all, and could not complain.

What is remarkable about both of these poets is that they should have been so sensitive to the horrors of war and critical of its management, and having been through hell once, yet they put themselves forward for another dose of the same medicine when they could have sat it out at home, secure in the knowledge that they had done their bit.

When Owen wrote *Dulce et Decorum Est,* from which the below comes, it did not come to him as a flash of inspiration scribbled down in haste:

> Gas! GAS! Quick, boys! – An ecstasy of fumbling,
> Fitting the clumsy helmets just in time;
> But someone still was yelling out and stumbling
> And flound'ring like a man in fire or lime…
> Dim, through the misty panes and thick green light,
> As under a green sea, I saw him drowning.
> In all my dreams, before my helpless sight,
> He plunges at me, guttering, choking, drowning.

It took hours of consideration, writing and rewriting as the correct version emerged. Sassoon was involved, as shown by the surviving manuscript with his annotations. Owen had been there and had relived the horrors during the Craiglockhart nights and when he was writing his poetry. Yet he still put himself forward.

That is courage.

Let us consider one of Sassoon's short poems:

The General

'Good-morning; good-morning!' the General said
When we met him last week on our way to the line.
Now the soldiers he smiled at are most of 'em dead,
And we're cursing his staff for incompetent swine.
'He's a cheery old card,' grunted Harry to Jack
As they slogged up to Arras with rifle and pack.
But he did for them both by his plan of attack.

It may not be the greatest of poetry – but it certainly packs a punch. Yet Sassoon volunteered to put himself once again at the mercy of others such as he.

That took courage.

Owen and Sassoon were together at Craiglockhart for no more than four months. Is it realistic to imagine that there could be tangible evidence remaining of their time together and their collaboration? What was Slateford Military Hospital is now a busy and cheerfully noisy place thronged with students as, behind the former hydro, Napier University has built an ultra-modern Business School. But the building's history is not forgotten, and the former entrance hall of the hydro is now home to the University's War Poets Collection and open to the public.

The district of Craiglockhart was mainly a bungaloid creation of the 1930s, with no village core. There is a parish church, a parade of shops, but no indication of community. But there is a Craiglockhart Community Council, and in 2012, with the Southwest Neighbourhood Partnership of the City of Edinburgh Council, they commissioned a sculpture called 'Hillside' by Lara Greene. PLATE 4B. The pharmacy and the post office are as close to a core as one could find in Craiglockhart and the sculpture shows, in green, with yellow leaves, the lower slopes of the ice-moulded Easter and Wester Craiglockhart Hills. The grey represents the basalt cliffs and the grey man 'silent upon a peak in Darien' must be Sassoon or Owen, alone but in tranquillity.

The panels in PLATE 5A, as well as recording the necessary credits, give quotations and explanations, like this:

[Owen] wrote 'Spring Offensive' after his experience of a disastrous attack in St Quentin in April 1917. He was diagnosed with shell shock in June and sent to the progressive Craiglockhart War Hospital for treatment.

This is clearly one of the most unusual Great War memorials we are likely to find and one wonders how the douce suburbanites of Craiglockhart have taken to it. A totally random approach to two residents of the area – probably younger than myself – evoked a miserable response.

Although Owen spent only three weeks at Tynecastle, he was not forgotten. Late in 1917, he used a few precious days' leave to revisit the school before returning to the Front. In one classroom, the English teacher, Mrs Fullerton, had written his army address on the blackboard and the class were making Christmas cards for him. This was to be Owen's last Christmas.

Tynecastle High School has not forgotten Owen either and did not require prompting from outside to make a contribution. The 1912 building is standing empty at the moment as it is caught up in plans to redevelop Tynecastle, the Heart of Midlothian football ground. A new school has been built and in 2008 there was an organised effort to place the 'Owen connection' as an inter-disciplinary effort in accordance with the Scottish Government's Curriculum for Excellence. School log books, newspapers and War Graves Commission records were researched.

On National Poetry Day, on the theme of Heroes and Heroines, pupils and staff took part in events involving art, history and school library staff. PC Cleghorn (ex-Royal Marine, Falklands), soldiers from the Royal Regiment of Scotland, and workers from the Poppy Scotland charity discussed their experiences in the Falklands, Iraq and Afghanistan and contemporary war poetry.

Pupils turned Owen's 'Dulce et Decorum Est' into an abstract piece of art that explored both the horrors of war and the heroism that can emerge in times of conflict. Another group used wordle.net (a website which creates artful 'word clouds' from text) to explore meaning behind the poetry of Owen, Sassoon, Isaac Rosenberg and others.

Owen's time at the school could have been left as a historical quirk, a surprising anecdote to trot out when showing visitors around the school. Instead, the chance encounter is collapsing the generational divide between a remote black-and-white war and 21st century teenagers.

CHAPTER 7

Memento Mori

I WAS FORTUNATE that both of my parents, each in a different way, fostered my natural curiosity and did not discourage exploration. One of my mother's contributions was a healthy appreciation of the interest and importance of cemeteries. Yet, even before going round the cemetery in a strange town or village, to see who had given their lives for King and country in 'the war to end all wars', it was necessary to inspect the war memorial. There was much to be learned about the town or parish from the listed names, dates and regiments.

As I said earlier, the proportion of Scots in the armed services was twice as great as for the rest of the United Kingdom, and the butcher's bill was also twice as high. Every part of the country was affected, but the long lists seem most poignant in what are now the empty places. Every death is a Sad Story, but the loss of, say, 20 men from a Highland glen, where the community itself was in danger of withering away, might seem to be more significant than the deaths of a hundred from the slums of Glasgow or Edinburgh.

In November 2006, I was making a kind of pilgrimage in the Gordon Highlanders country of Aberdeenshire and Banffshire. Here there are dozens of villages, each with its war memorial, and rural crossroads in small parishes, with lists and lists and lists of young men who left the peewits' cry of their countryside forever.

In the years between the Boer War and the Great War – in both of which he fought – my grandfather was the postie in The Cabrach. In Groome's *Ordnance Gazetteer of Scotland* of 1882, The Cabrach is described as a large parish of over 50 square miles, 'prevailingly mountainous, pastoral and bleak'. The lowest point in the parish was 800 feet and the population – in 1881 – was a mere 682 and falling.

For some reason, his years in The Cabrach ranked high in my grandfather's memory, and when I was young he would regale me with the characteristics of every croft and farm and his heroic ventures during the fierce winters. Global warming was not even a concept in the early 20th century. The Cabrach is empty now, and all that remains are the names on an old map and a few ruined gable ends of cottages.

Recently, BBC Scotland's countryside programme *Landward* used The Cabrach as a case study of the impact of the Great War on the Scottish countryside. Apart from the gross error of giving the population of the pre-war Cabrach as over 2,000, this programme portrayed very well the struggles of a community whose young men had gone 'aff to fecht or fa'', leaving the women, children and old men to reap the scanty crops and mind the wandering sheep. The winter of 1915 was abnormally severe, even for The Cabrach, and there was real poverty and shortage of food. The result was that people just gave up, abandoned their holdings and moved down to the comparative security of Dufftown, Huntly and Rhynie.

Rural depopulation is a worldwide phenomenon and has many causes, of which war is only one. One thinks of 1815, when the Gordon Highlanders, who had behaved so heroically at Waterloo were discharged at Portsmouth and had to walk back to their homes – to find that they had been destroyed and their families cleared off the land for sheep. The survivors of 1919 must have had similar thoughts when they came back to the 'land fit for heroes'.

Tarland is a large village with the war memorial in the middle of the square. A few yards away, Tarland's biggest shop had one of its large plate glass windows given over to an Armistice Day display, with photographs, documents and several kilts – the 'yellow thread in the Gordon plaid' – prominent.

The saddest story implied on the monument dates from the Second World War. Lady MacRobert's three sons all served – and died – in the RAF. Her reaction to this family tragedy was to buy a bomber, donate it to the RAF, and have it named 'MacRobert's Reply'.

Some memorials display a savage irony. In 2004 in South Uist, and in 2005 in Harris, during the intervals between climbing the extremely rugged mountains, I noted something odd about the war memorials. The dates of the Great War were given as from 1914 to 1919. Now, we know that the 11th day of the 11th month of 1918 was only an Armistice, a cease fire, and not the formal end of the war – but nobody else in Britain seems to have acknowledged this. But 1919 in the Outer Hebrides refers to a terrible and avoidable loss of life among a group who had every reason to feel euphoric at having got through the greatest struggle in Europe up to that date.

In 1968, Francis Thompson wrote in *Lewis and Harris*:

Those in Harris and Lewis aged 50 or over have their recollections charged with little else but disaster. Not only did the island lose an abnormally high percentage of its young men in the 1914 war, but some 200 of those who survived the holocaust were lost in the wreck of the *Iolaire* on New Year's morning, 1919 – the first morning of the first new year of peace, literally within sight of home.

HMS *Iolaire* was an Admiralty yacht which was bringing sailors back from the war to their homes on Lewis. She left the railhead of Kyle of Lochalsh in poor visibility and deteriorating weather on the evening of 31 December 1918. She was expected at Stornoway and there was therefore a good turnout of wives and children waiting to welcome their loved ones home. Instead, they had the doubtful pleasures of watching their sons and fathers drowning little more than a stone's throw from the shore and finding their men washed up on the shore the next day.

Because, at 2.30am on New Year's Day, as the ship approached the port of Stornoway, a few yards offshore and a mile away from the safety of Stornoway Harbour, she hit the infamous rocks 'The Beasts of Holm', and eventually sank. The sailors were wearing their full uniforms including heavy boots, so swimming from the wreck was difficult – even for the few who had had the opportunity to learn.

The final death toll was officially put at 205, of whom 181 were islanders, but as the ship was badly overcrowded and there was a lack of proper records, the death toll could have been slightly higher. John F Macleod, from Ness in Lewis saved 40 lives, swimming ashore with a heaving line, along which many of the survivors made their way to safety. Only 75 of the 280 (officially known) passengers survived the disaster, 73 per cent perished in the incident.

This was the worst peacetime disaster involving a British ship since the RMS *Titanic* on 15 April 1912.

The jury at the Court of Inquiry found

That the *Iolaire* went ashore and was wrecked on the rocks inside the 'Beasts of Holm' (outside Stornoway) about 1.55am on the morning of 1 January, resulting in the death of 205 men; that the officers in charge did not exercise sufficient prudence in approaching the harbour; that the boat did not slow down, and that the look-out was not on duty at the time of the accident; that the number of lifeboats, boats and rafts was insufficient for the number of people carried, and that no orders were given by the officers with a view to saving life; and, further, that there was a valuable time between the signals of distress and the arrival of life-saving apparatus in the vicinity of the wreck.

The findings of the Court generated much ill feeling amongst the Lewis population with accusations of a 'whitewash'. While drunkenness among the crew was discounted at the enquiry, the suspicion has never gone away.

The most remote war memorial must be the one above Glencoul in North-West Sutherland. The North-West of Scotland is the most incredible maelstrom of landscape in these islands. In his *Hutton's Arse,* Malcolm Rider covers 'three billion years of extraordinary geology in Scotland's Northern Highlands'. Inchnadamph is known to geologists all over the world as the base from which Ben Peach and John Horne spent 15 years unravelling the secrets of this area – and the task continues to this day.

Most travellers drive through this area unconscious of its geological uniqueness – but can still be overwhelmed by the splendid savagery of the wild loch and mountain scenery. Out of the Lewisian gneiss rises an array of fantastic peaks with names like Stac Polly, Suilven, Quinag, Canisp, although only two of them are over 3,000 feet. Rider sees them as giant chess pieces on a board of ice – polished gneiss. Seen from the north on an angry day the northern sandstone buttresses of Quinag are, quite simply, terrifying.

Water is everywhere. What human settlement as there is can be found mainly along the inhospitable rocky coast, but Eddrachillis Bay is dotted with a myriad of tiny islands. Conversely, the land is dotted with a number of larger lochs and a myriad of little lochans, with a confused system of streams linking them. There are also waterfalls – including Eas a' Chual Aluinn, the highest in Britain at 638 feet. There is no visitor centre here, no café, scarcely a footpath.

Several saltwater lochs run eastward into the land. One is Loch a' Chairn Bhain, which runs for about five miles to narrows at Kylesku, where for many years there was a free but frustrating ferry for vehicles using the A894, the road serving the West of Sutherland. Now there is a splendid corniche-type road with a superb curved bridge, contrasting with the wild amphitheatre around. Standing on the bridge we can see:

> To the east the waters of Loch Glendhu and Loch Glencoul penetrate deep into the wild and roadless hills in the manner of Norwegian fjords.

Loch Glencoul is about four miles long and from its head a walk of another mile takes one to a point from which the full height of the Eas a' Chual Aluinn can be seen.

Near the shore at the head of the loch is Glencoul, a cottage only accessible by a long trek over rough country or a boat trip up the loch. Today it is empty. Before the Great War it was the home of the Elliot family. High above the cottage, shining bright on a sunny day, is a white marble memorial cross – surely the most isolated of its kind in the country.

John and Margaret Elliot moved into the two-storey house after shepherd John took a job as a deer stalker on the sprawling Reay estate, now part of the Reay Forest Estate. The sons whose names are on the cross were William, who was born on 7 November 1891, and Alistair on 11 November 1892. They had three brothers: Matthew, born in 1896, John David, born in 1898 and James, born in 1901. The house where the brothers grew up was so remote that, rather than having them travel miles to school, the Duke of Westminster – who owned the estate – arranged for a small school house to be built on to the side of their family cottage, including a room for the teacher to live in.

William Elliot was a stalker on the Reay estate and served as a corporal in the Camerons, in France and at Gallipoli. He had been serving with the 2nd Entrenching Battalion, a holding unit for men returning to the trenches after being in hospital, when he was taken ill, dying of pneumonia, aged 25, in March 1917. Alistair was a Lance-corporal in the Highland Light Infantry and had been a bank clerk in Glasgow at the outbreak of war. He was killed in action in Belgium in April 1918, aged 24. He was one of those whose body was never recovered. Matthew was in the Lovat Scouts (an elite snipers' unit recruited from the Highland gillies and stalkers). He was gassed and suffered in the years after. John David was also in the Camerons, was wounded and carried a piece of shrapnel in his face for the rest of his life. The youngest son, James, escaped harm, as he was born in 1901 and was too young to serve.

The monument was paid for by the Duke of Westminster of the time and carries the brothers' names – William and Alistair. Below, the inscription reads: 'Their memory will ever be cherished by their sorrowing parents and brothers.' Alistair's name was misspelt by the stonemason who carved the stone, but what matters is that he is remembered – few passers-by will notice the error.

The house at Glencoul has been empty for many years, but the school house on the side is used and maintained by the Mountain Bothies Association – a very appropriate use for a building in such a place. Just a few years ago, the existing Duke of Westminster paid for the marble to be repaired after a few cracks appeared.

Speaking before Remembrance Day in 2012, the soldiers' nephew Willie Elliot, 79, himself a veteran of the Korean War, said:

> It is very easy to get emotional when you are up there and see their memorial sitting in such a remote but beautiful place. Brothers William and Alistair Elliot grew up in the now empty estate cottage that lies in the shadow of the memorial. As young boys, the sound of their laughter and voices once filled the glen. But even living so far away from everything didn't mean the war did not reach them.

What on earth had the death of yet another Hapsburg in central Europe to do with folks like the Elliots of Glencoul?

Seventy miles south, at Glenelg, there could hardly be a greater contrast. Glenelg is a huge parish with an area of two 200 square miles, not acres or hectares. It is mountainous, 'with strikingly grand scenery' and has the big sea lochs Morar and Nevis. There are four hills of over 3,000 feet and a tangle of lesser summits. 'Freshwater lakes are numerous'. 'The inhabitants… are mostly congregated along the coasts' where the ones who were not shipped off to Canada were dumped when cleared off the glens of the 'wild and inhospitable interior'.

But the real contrast is between the war memorials. Glencoul's is simple and modest – but not cheap – while that by the shore at Glenelg is outrageous. Access to Glenelg is over the Mam Ratagan, an old military road where Dr Johnson had a worrying few minutes in 1773. Just beyond Glenelg village, next to Kyle Rhea, the channel between the mainland and Skye, one turns a corner to be knocked over by the most grandiose of sculptured groups. It would not be out of place in a big French provincial town, but here, with the sea and the hills of Skye beyond, it is a display of panache in the face of sorrow. PLATE 5B.

A winged Victory, with her laurel wreath, rises from the debris of a broken drum, a discarded knapsack, a broken crown and a tentative dove of peace. She towers over a superbly constructed maiden ('Stricken Humanity') who reaches up to Victory's graciously extended hand. Meanwhile, a moustachioed Highlander, accoutred in kilt, Balmoral and puttees, with ammunition pouches and a tin hat, modestly averts his eyes from the unseemly display of abundant female flesh.

The 1920s were a boom time for sculptors, and as a result most Great War memorials are fairly conventional in their design and arrangement. With so many being commissioned at the same time it is no surprise to find standard designs with long lists on the sides of a large block on whose top glowers a resolute Highlander or a sturdy infantryman with puttees and a fixed bayonet. This is why the Glenelg monument is so refreshing.

The roll of those who gave their lives is also unusual. Of the 16 from World War I (four from World War II) only six were from local regiments, five from the Camerons and one Seaforth. Two were from the Canadians and there was a New Zealander – presumably men who had emigrated from Glenelg before 1914 but had joined up to come back to Europe to serve the country of their birth. There were two Captains from the 7th Battalion of the Queen's Regiment (the 2nd of Foot, based in Surrey) and two from the cavalry. Major Valentine Fleming was from the Oxfordshire Yeomanry and his name and presence among the dead provide an explanation for this exotic display of grief and gratitude in such an unlikely place.

Valentine Fleming (1882–1917) was the son of Robert Fleming, a wealthy Scottish banker. The Flemings were big landowners in the parish of Glenelg. Fleming also had an estate at Huntercombe, in Oxfordshire, which accounts for the cavalry connection, and was MP for Henley from 1910 till his death. Fleming was killed on 20 May 1917, was awarded a posthumous DSO and was the subject of an appreciation in *The Times* by Winston Churchill.

Major Fleming's widow – Evelyn St Croix Rose Fleming – inherited the large estate in trust, which made her a very wealthy woman. Should she ever remarry, the trust would cut her out, thus ensuring that she would remain forever a widow, regardless of other loves or circumstances (she and Fleming had been married on St Valentine's Day). Her older son, Peter (1907–71), acquired some celebrity as a traveller in Brazil and Central Asia and served with distinction in the Second World War. One of his travel books was made a home reader in some of our more forward-looking post-war schools, but he is pretty well forgotten today.

Her younger son, Ian, (1908–64) grew up in the shadow of his brilliant brother and had a rather unsatisfactory career until, in 1952, his character James Bond appeared in *Casino Royale* and – as they say – the rest is history.

With a background like hers, it is not surprising that the widow would not be content with the usual workmanlike monument.

Another big landowner was Lady Scott, mother of the Captain Scott on the monument, who wished to commemorate her son. The people of Glenelg were given the choice of a memorial or a new – much-needed – pier. That they chose the former tells us a lot about the spirit of the times.

Sir Robert Lorimer designed the memorial. Louis Reid Deuchars modelled the sculpture which was cast in London, to become one of the most striking and spectacular war memorials in Scotland (its picture graces the cover of *Scotland's First World War* by Kevin Munro, published by Historic Scotland in Edinburgh in 2014.)

Another remote memorial testifies to the fact that some communities did not forget their dead, or need a distant Prime Minister to jog their memories. Hard by the A863 on the west side of Skye the map indicates an 'Other Tourist Feature'. On the ground, this turns out to be a memorial to the dead of wars, erected in 1987. Bracadale is hardly even a township, but when the road was straightened the space between the old and new roads became a kind of community focus, with new houses, a café/book-shop and an outdoors shop.

The Memorial is a simple column of local stone, with a plaque listing the names – a roll call of Highland names, regiments and years of death. PLATE 6A. Unusually, almost as many died in the Second World War as in the First. Also unusual, perhaps unique, is that the memorial is enclosed within a roughly crenellated square wall, reminiscent of a sheep fold.

On the crenellations are small plaques giving detailed information – illustrated – about each of the local lads who fell. They are not forgotten in Bracadale.

Fiction is often better at catching a mood or an emotion than a straightforward narrative. Arbuthnot, in what used to be Kincardineshire, is a small rural parish with a modest kirk and kirkyard. In it is a simple stone, now decaying, 'for the memory of James Leslie Mitchell (Lewis Grassic Gibbon)', with his dates. On the village hall, the old school, a few yards away, is a plain, simple, but quite remarkable plaque.

As the granite memorials of Aberdeenshire reflect the land from which those who died came – hard, dour, but enduring – and Glenelg commemorates the rich and hierarchical providers of its grandiose monument, so Arbuthnot embodies the intimate relationship between its people and the land.

Most memorials list the dead in military fashion, by reference to the units they served in. The arrangement is usually hierarchical – senior officers at the top, down to the privates, gunners, sappers, seamen or whatever at the bottom or round the sides. Decorations are usually listed.

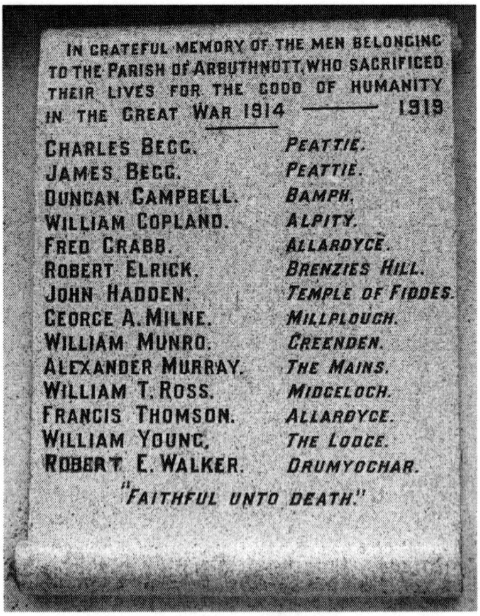

At Arbuthnott, however, the arrangement is quite simple – names in egalitarian alphabetical order down the left hand side and opposite each name the place, farm or croft, he originated from. The dedication is:

Fig 10 'Faithful unto Death' – Arbuthnott War Memorial
Walter M Stephen

> In grateful memory of the men belonging to the Parish of Arbuthnott who sacrificed their lives for the good of humanity in the Great War 1914–1919.

Again, the egalitarian touch. These men did not die for a far-off King or an amorphous Commonwealth but for a simpler noble ideal. The good of humanity is above jingoism.

It can be no coincidence that Lewis Grassic Gibbon should be buried a few yards off. No writer has better expressed than he the love-hate relationship between the peasant and the land, particularly in *Sunset Song*. It begins with a wonderful survey of sequent occupance, tracing the story of the Kinraddie lands from the time of the Picts. Through the medium of a young Chris Guthrie, there is brought out the struggle between the desire for material advancement and gentrification, and the primal pull of the land, the soil, the language and the folk memory.

The last few pages describe the unveiling of the Kinraddie memorial. The locals thought that the minister would

Have a fine stone angel, with a night-gown on, raised up at Kinraddie cross-roads.

(perhaps a cheaper version of the Glenelg memorial).
Instead, he:

Had the old stone circle by Blawearie loch raised up and cleaned and set all in place, real heathen-like.

On the day, the minister preached from the text: 'For I will give you the Morning Star', reminding the folk present of those who had gone 'from the lands they loved' that they were: 'the Last of the Peasants, the last of the Old Scots folk'. Although they had died for a world that was past they had not died for the world 'we seem to inherit'. Instead he saw: 'a greater hope and a newer world undreamt when these four died'. Then occurred a scene familiar and moving to people of my generation.

The Highland man McIvor tuned up his pipes and began to step slow round the stone circle by Blawearie Loch: slow and quiet, and folk watched him, the dark was near, it lifted your hair and was eerie and uncanny, the *Flowers of the Forest* as he played it. It rose and wept and cried, that crying for the men that fell in battle... He fair could play, the piper, he tore at your heart marching there with the tune leaping up the moor and echoing across the loch.

As night falls, the Kinraddie folk disperse, and we are left with Chris and the minister looking to a future together.

A monument must record the best about the whole messy business. Dying for the good of humanity will seem naïve to many observers. The minister, in his address, strikes a note of ambiguity which resonates better to those of us with the gift of hindsight. The only thing that does not ring true about this last scene from *Sunset Song* is that there are only four names on the Kinraddie memorial – even a little parish like Arbuthnot had 12 and most had dozens, or even hundreds.

CHAPTER 8

Their Name Liveth

IN JULY 2013, I was diagnosed with the fifth commonest type of cancer in the UK, in an aggressive form. Fortunately, I was in Phase I and was put on a 'curative' programme. Because of two possible complications, I was kept under observation and free from possible infections in Ward 8 of the Western General Hospital, Edinburgh, for two weeks.

This was an interesting experience, in that I did not feel particularly unwell – on admission, the nurse who documented me said I was the healthiest patient she had ever seen there! – but I was in the midst of a group of people at all stages of the disease. At times I felt quite guilty, as I had a room to myself and was able to bounce around cheerily while their situations were much worse than mine.

One solution was to get out of the ward as much as possible, popping down to the shop for the paper, going down to one of the gardens to do my morning exercises – and just exploring. I had been in and out, up and down, the Western General several times without seeing it as anything more than a huge collection of buildings, many of them looking disturbingly temporary. In *The Buildings of Scotland: Edinburgh*, Colin McWilliam says:

> The history of post-1945 hospital architecture is... marred by a policy that took the worst of both worlds, retaining old buildings but subjecting them to piecemeal extension with a defiance of their character that often seems deliberate.

he describes the Western General as having 'conscientious architecture, but mostly at cross purposes, adding up to a tangled makeshift'.

I made it my business to see whether I could – for my own satisfaction – make sense of the institutional hotch-potch around me.

It was easy to find the buildings which formed the core of the Western General. Flanked by giant cedars and chestnut trees are great three-decker sandstone blocks, by Peddie and Kinnear, reputable Edinburgh architects, with an imposing entrance and a splendid clock tower – with a working clock. (Rather charmingly, the clock is still working, but to its own rhythm, so that it never shows the correct time, nor does it show a constant relationship with the rest of Britain.) This was the Poor House (in Scotland, we did not have workhouses) of the parishes of St Cuthbert's and Canongate, built in 1867, and catering for the western districts of Edinburgh and the eastern part of the Old Town. In 1927 it was turned into a hospital and from the 1950s became the core of an ever-increasing complex of specialist buildings.

In 1867 this was a greenfield site, well away from the infections and evils of the city. A small early 19th century development out in the fields, called Comely Bank, set off a process of gentrification of the neighbourhood, which Homer Hoyt would have seen as a wedge of middle class or upper class development in his theory of urban growth. In 1843, a private Comely Bank Cemetery was opened and in 1898 it was bought by the Edinburgh Cemetery Company, who had it extended and laid out by JM Dick Peddie. Fettes College (1864–70) arrived to the east of the Poor House. A tram service was started from Princes Street to a terminus just outside the cemetery, where was built Flora Stevenson School, an Edinburgh Board School triple-decker, named after the redoubtable Chairman of the Board. Edinburgh, at that time, was a pioneer in the treatment of consumption (tuberculosis) and, next to the cemetery, two conversions, five new buildings and a 'swanky' administration block were put together over the period 1894–1906 to form the Royal Victoria Hospital.

By the second Sunday of my stay in Ward 8, I had exhausted the attractions of the Western General. I knew the area well, but had never been in the cemetery. This would be a good time to fill in this gap in my experience.

The story of Edinburgh's private cemeteries has been a public scandal, although the City authorities have now stabilised the situation – albeit in a miserable financial climate. Comely Bank is not at all bad. Nicely laid out with paths and a modest central focus, it is reasonably well-kept in a minimalist kind of way, and with a decent, but not outstanding, cross-section of middle-class Edinburgh.

Getting up the very modest slope at the back I noticed a biggish flat-topped grassy mound, obviously not new. It was a mass grave and a few minutes later, I came across a formal war cemetery with an information board put up by the Commonwealth War Graves Commission. But why here, in peaceful suburbia hundreds of miles from the guns and the gas?

During the Great War, this plot was bought from the Edinburgh

Cemetery Company for the dead from three institutions which were brigaded together as the 2nd Scottish General Hospital. Craigleith Poorhouse held over 1,000 officers and men. Leith Infirmary, which had become Leith War Hospital, had 585. About 12 miles west of Edinburgh, in West Lothian, was Bangour Village Hospital, built as a lunatic asylum for the City of Edinburgh in 1898–1906. It was taken over as a War Hospital in 1915 and by 1918 had 3,000 patients.

At least 225 men were buried at Comely Bank – and two women, presumably auxiliaries. In addition, at least 50 died in the Spanish flu pandemic which swept across Europe early in 1919 and which may have killed more than the war itself. It is so ironic and tragic that these fellows must have been so badly wounded that they were still in hospital after the war's end – but felt safe, only to be swept away by an alien infection. My little sojourn, trivial compared with theirs, gave me an empathy for their plight I might not have otherwise felt.

Comely Bank is one of the 12,500 locations maintained by the Commonwealth War Graves Commission throughout the United Kingdom. It is very well-kept, is well designed and has its own individuality. We are familiar with the standard CWGC gravestone of Portland stone, set in seemingly interminable rows 'in Flanders' fields'. In Comely Bank we see the hand of Sir Robert Lorimer, who designed the layout and the non-standard gravestones. These are granite panels, flat on the ground like the graves of the Scottish kings at Iona. Each panel gives the names, numbers, regiments, regimental badges and dates of death of five or six soldiers. PLATE 6B. Does this symbolise comradeship, even unto death? Eight New Zealanders, seven Australians and 11 Canadians are also grouped together in death, reminding us that this was a World War.

Browsing around one is struck by the number of those who lingered on in hospital long after the Armistice – for example, 5 June 1921 (Machine Gun Corps), 19 January 1920 (Middlesex Regiment), 9 January 1920 (Highland Light Infantry), 30 August 1921. There was a cluster of deaths from 9 February to 12 February 1919. Spanish flu? Four Canadians died between 24 February and 1 March 1919. The flu again?

Elsewhere in the cemetery there is the occasional standard war grave. One is for SQMS Frederick Fox, 9th Queen's Royal Lancers, who died at the Castle Hospital, Edinburgh, on 29 January 1933, aged 39 years. RIP. 'This stone was erected by his comrades in the regiment'. Several questions arise, but at least we know that he was buried here because – illogical though it may seem – Edinburgh Castle is in the parish of Canongate, not Edinburgh.

Another True Story must lie behind S/55, the gravestone of a Lady Driver. She was Jeanie LL Cockburn, of the Women's Legion, who was attached to the Royal Army Service Corps and who died on 15 December 1918 – a month after the Armistice – aged 20. The pity of it all.

'Their Name Liveth for Evermore'. True or false? Certainly, in Comely Bank Cemetery, there is no excuse for forgetting.

The South Side in Edinburgh is another of Homer Hoyt's sectors of middle class or upper class development, reinforcing his theory of urban growth. From the little New Town of George Square run two or three great main roads, lined with Georgian terraced houses, and then big Victorian villas, out to Newington and the University's Kings Buildings.

In 1848 – five years after Comely Bank – Newington, also a private cemetery, was opened. It was a cut above Comely Bank, with an impressive gatehouse, a semi-formal layout, a terrace and catacombs. It is surrounded by a high wall so that, for years, I thought there might be something of interest here without bothering to investigate further.

Eventually, spurred on by the search for McCrae's Battalion, I ventured through the gates to find that Newington Cemetery was one of those private cemeteries in Edinburgh which have been systematically neglected. Stones have been tumbled and, although the cemetery has been taken over by the City, maintenance is minimal.

Along the east side is a large plot, bounded by a set of broken railings, which was the former 'Jewish quarter' of the city. Surprisingly, this area is in depressing disarray, with broken and decaying stones and an air of total neglect.

Fairly close to the main gate is the highest point and most formal section of the cemetery – and the grandest stones. Moving downhill we find what looks like a mass grave. Nearby is a large monument headed 'Their Name Liveth for Evermore' and bearing lists of names from the 1914–18 War. From the monument, we learn that 139 British soldiers and sailors were buried in this cemetery, 53 of them in the adjacent plot, and 12 are not recorded elsewhere.

Moving down the cemetery, near the lowest corner, far from the entrance gate, one begins to notice, here and there, the characteristic stones of

World War 1 graves. Some lie with their families, like Lieutenant Macintosh, who was killed two days before the Armistice. The Witherspoons lie together. Private Witherspoon of the Royal Scots died on 2 May 1918. His daughter Maggie died on 9 November 1918, two days before the Armistice. His widow, Christina, died in 1959, after 41 years as a widow.

There is something odd about these graves and the modest concentration at the bottom corner. PLATE 7A. Here are not the serried ranks of stones of France or Flanders, beautifully maintained, with large numbers from one unit which was at the heart of the action. Over at the other side of the city, at Comely Bank, all was as it should be. But down here, in the out-of-the-way corner, all is untidy, unkempt and, it must be said, forgotten.

The poor fellows who lie in Newington came from a great variety of units – the Royal Scots (the local regiment), Camerons, Argylls, Royal Scots Fusiliers, West Yorkshires, Middlesex Regiment, Royal Engineers.

There is even a Stoker First Class from the Navy.

What is noteworthy is when some of these fellows died – Stoker First Class Hastie on 17 January 1919, Private McGinty on 4 February 1919, Private Trainer on 12 February 1919, Private Boyd on 14 March 1919, Sapper Campbell on 22 March 1919, Private McLaren on 2 April 1919 and Private Purdie on 22 April 1921.

Newington was like Comely Bank, in that it was the nearest cemetery to a military hospital during World War 1. Mr JA Longmore left £10,000 to found an Edinburgh Hospital for incurables in 1874. The 'solemnly classical' sandstone building, with pilasters and Doric columns (by JM Dick Peddie of St Cuthbert's Poorhouse and Comely Bank cemetery) was formally opened in 1880. On average, it held 100 patients, 40 of them natives of Edinburgh, each with about 1,100 cubic feet of space.

During the Great War, the Longmore Hospital was turned over for use as a military hospital and inevitably many died there. Many of them must have been so badly wounded that they hovered between life and death for a time after the war ended – in Private Purdie's case for over two years. What sad stories lie behind the neat inscriptions? Two of the dead were from the RAMC, one of them Private Briggs who died on 4 May 1915, aged only 17, and Private Wilson. They may well have died of some infection caught from their patients.

In particular, this little group of stones is a simple reminder that the horrors of war last longer than its battles and glories.

One last comparison. On the Comely Bank picture, a modest little shrine can be seen, just beyond the information board. On its north face is a small cupboard with a metal door, in which there is a detailed roll of all those buried here. There is no such thing at Newington. One has to ask: 'Why not?'

'Their Name Liveth?' It all depends, doesn't it?

CHAPTER 9

Observe the Sons of Ulster

IT IS A CHARMING quirk of Ulster urbanism that the central square of most of the planned towns of that province is called 'The Diamond' but is, in fact, a square. Londonderry is no exception. From four gates in the city walls, Ferryquay Street, Shipquay Street, Bishop Street and Butcher Street lead straight to the centre where, instead of a crossroads there is a sizeable square – The Diamond. In the middle of The Diamond is the Diamond War Memorial, a dignified column surmounted by a winged Victory, holding aloft in her right hand a triumphant laurel wreath. Her left hand holds a lowered sword, no longer needed. She has two fine bronze supporters at the base of the column. A resolute soldier with puttees is about to bayonet with a backhand thrust a wounded foe. Sailors do not normally appear on war memorials but the other supporter is a splendid sailor in a gale, with bare feet on a slippery deck and trousers rolled up.

The inscription on the Memorial now reads:

To Our Honoured Dead
And Those Who Served
1914–1918
1939–1945

Long before the Holy Alliance of the Prime Minister, Lord Ashcroft and the *Daily Telegraph* decided to commemorate the First World War, the people of Londonderry launched their Diamond War Memorial Project to commemorate the 90th anniversary of the ending of the Great War and the 80th anniversary of the opening of the Diamond War Memorial on 23 June 1927.

Fig 11 The Diamond War Memorial – the Soldier
Walter M Stephen

The result was a substantial *Commemorative Diary 2008* on heavy paper, with a ring binding and a cover silhouette of the winged Victory on top of the Diamond War Memorial. PLATE 7B. This excellent *Diary* is built around the 756 individuals who died during the Great War and whose names were recorded on the Memorial. The project also researched 400 additional individuals who died during that conflict but had birth, work, education, family and historic ties to the city.

The form of the *Diary* is quite simple. There is a page for every day of the year and on each page are recorded the names, rank and numbers of those who were killed on that day. Thus on 1 September three were killed in 1914, one in 1915 and five in 1918. There were quiet days – no-one was killed on 25, 26 or 27 December. But there were busy days too.

For example, for 21 March there is a little caption at the top of the page:

March 21 – April 5 1918. The Kaiserschlacht offensive pushes the British back 40 miles, but cannot be supported.

And there follow 20 names of those from this city that died on that day, followed by a photograph of Lance Corporal Charles H Dooley in uniform. Eighteen died the following day. There are many short entries about individuals, usually stating where they came from, their local connection and how they died.

One in seven of those who died did so on a single day – 1 July 1916.

Private James (Jim) Gamble, 12701 was one of the 113 killed on 1 July. His was certainly a sad story:

He was the son of Alexander and Jane Gamble, 1 Lower Ebrington Street, Waterside, Londonderry, and a member of Londonderry City Mission Clooney Hall Methodist Church. His name is recorded on the Thiepval Memorial to the Missing, Somme, France and commemorated on the Diamond War Memorial.

As James Gamble lay dying, he wrote a heartfelt farewell message on the covers of a couple of little Wesleyan Hymn books, which had been given to him by the Reverend Robert Byers.

On the carton holding the books was the direction, 'Please send these to Mr and Mrs A Gamble, 1 Ebrington Street, Londonderry.'

The little package, all bloodstained, was found by a Lieutenant Hales lying at the bottom of a trench quite close to the body of the Derry man.

The first part of Private Gamble's message read:

'From Jim – Dear Father and Mother. I have done my best and I hope to meet you in Heaven. God bless you.'

On the second book was written:

'Please do not weep for me. I shall be happy to the last. With love and kisses. – Jim.'

Private Jim Gamble was the sole support of his mother, his father being paralysed and his brother, in the Garrison Artillery, married. He served his apprenticeship in Ebrington Factory, and was a collar cutter in Leeds when the King's call for men came to him.

Other such stories can be guessed at by such headings as 'First local casualty of the Great War', 'Thompson trio tragedy', 'Conflict claims life of young bandsman', 'Hero leads attack', 'Patriotism, like love, is self-sacrifice'. Tillie and Henderson was the biggest shirt factory in the world and 'A family at war' describes how the conflict cost the lives of three of the immediate family and another four closely connected through marriage. Without question many of the other dead would have been former employees of Tillie's. The Roll of Honour for Welch Margetson & Co Ltd, another shirt factory, shows that 122 of their staff volunteered for military service.

There are numerous full page entries of a more general nature. The frontispiece is a photo of the opening of the Memorial on 23 June 1927. A poster shows an Irish piper with an Irish wolfhound and the caption – "The Call to Arms – Irishmen, don't you hear it?' A copy of a post card shows a trooper seated on a rock in front of a tented encampment, using his flat cap to write 'We are doing our duty at Londonderry'. Full page photos and sketches of all aspects of the military life punctuate the passing months.

As the first day of a month, the First of July rates a fine sketch of the Sons of Ulster going over the top. Three pages are necessary to deal with this day, the first day of the Battle of the Somme, which has already been covered in earlier chapters, but which has the greatest significance for those in Northern Ireland.

The First of July was already a special day, a day full of symbols, songs and slogans for the Sons of Ulster. In 1688 the Catholic James VII of Scotland and II of England was driven from his throne and replaced by the Protestants William and Mary. James still had a presence and an army in

Ireland and went to war against what he saw as dissident subjects in the north of that island.

As James's army approached the walled city of Londonderry, 12 *Prentice Boys* closed the city's gates against their royal master. And so began *The Siege of Derry*. It was long and hard and miserable and at one point the besiegers offered to end the siege. *'No Surrender'* came back the defiant reply. Eventually, *The Maiden City* was relieved when the *Mountjoy* sailed up the Foyle, breaking the boom across the river.

William of Orange brought over an army, landing at *Carrickfergus*. He advanced towards Dublin till the two armies faced each other across the *River Boyne*. At the end of the day (1st July Old Style), *King Billy on his white horse* rode through the waters of the river and through the shattered remnants of James's army.

From that day, *Remember 1690* has been the slogan and the anniversary has been commemorated by parades of bands playing such stirring tunes as 'Derry's Walls', 'The Protestant Boys' and 'On the Green Grassy Slopes of the Boyne' and heading up banners displaying the symbols of the resistance to absolute and capricious monarchy.

Briefly, the Ulster Division began the day well, but was held up by the British barrage allowing German reinforcements to be brought up. But they drove in for three-quarters of a mile near Thiepval. However, the units on either side had been less successful and the Ulstermen found themselves attacked from three sides, to end up in the evening where they had started off in the morning.

> Understandably, therefore, the Ulster Division counted 1 July a victory and the date... is observed by the Protestants of the province as one of their holy days.

The Ulster Division was the only division of X Corps to have achieved its objectives on the opening day of the battle. This came at a heavy price, with the division suffering in two days of fighting 5,500 officers and men killed, wounded or missing. War correspondent Philip Gibbs said of the Division: 'Their attack was one of the finest displays of human courage in the world'. Of nine Victoria Crosses given to British forces in the battle, four were awarded to 36th Division soldiers.

The *Diary* records that many who were to die on 1 July 1916 were church members, members of masonic and Orange Lodges, even members of flute bands. They must have been fully conscious of their heritage and associated their present struggle with that heritage. That heritage demanded that they be 'determined to follow the stern path of duty'.

However, Frank McGuiness, who received the (London) Evening Standard Award for Most Promising Playwright, for his gripping 1985 play *Observe the Sons of Ulster Marching Towards the Somme,* demonstrated that the reality of the situation was more complex than this simple message of 'Remember 1690'. His play has several themes, including homosexuality, homophobia and the inner conflicts of self-respect, bravery and patriotism.

Scrutiny of the individual items in the *Diary* reveals some interesting angles. Politics in Londonderry has always been ferocious. Hogg of Hogg and Mitchell was a successful industrialist, Lord Lieutenant of the County – and a Home Ruler. His opponents campaigned against him with the slogan: 'Hogg in the river, with a knife in his liver' – and meant it!

In and around Derry was a lively nationalist presence and many were members of the Irish National Volunteers. At the outbreak of war they were encouraged to support the British war effort and join Irish regiments of Kitchener's New Army. From the whole of Ireland 175,000 of the INV left to join up, leaving 13,500 behind to subvert actively the British presence in Ireland. Most of the Derry Men of Ulster joined the Royal Inniskilling Fusiliers, the Royal Irish Rifles or the Royal Ulster Rifles which formed the 36th (Ulster) Division. However, the 8th Battalion Royal Inniskilling Fusiliers formed part of the largely Catholic and Nationalist 16th (Irish) Division.

Many represented on the Memorial had been in the INV, one had even played in the Owen Roe O'Neill Band. Not uncommon in the *Diary* are references to 'a Catholic soldier', 'a very devoted Catholic' or the last rites being administered by a Catholic priest. Second Lieutenant Charles Love Crockett died as a result of 'friendly fire' during the Easter Rising.

Willie Doherty was killed in action at Gallipoli in 1915. His brother Bernard was gassed and wounded but survived the Great War, only to be shot in Orchard Street in 1920 'during a lull in riotous firing'. He staggered to Linenhall Street, where he fell. The Reverend L Hegarty administered the last rites, and ten minutes later Doherty expired. It was decided not to acquaint his mother of the tragedy, owing to the delicate state of her health.

From the *Diary* it is clear that a large number of men enlisted on the mainland, especially in the Scottish Regiments. Some may, of course, have been working in Scotland but there is much evidence to suggest that Ulstermen crossed the North Channel so that their families would not face reprisals back home. Port Glasgow, Greenock, Glasgow, Clydebank, Ayr, Govan, Perth and even Kinlochleven, Lancaster and Crewe saw Derrymen joining up.

The only woman was Nurse Laura Marion Gailey, Voluntary Aid Detachment (VAD) who died on 24 March 1917 in the City Hospital, Liverpool. A dedicated Unionist, she served in a military hospital, contracted measles and died of pneumonia. She had a funeral with the band and buglers of the Welsh Fusiliers and full military honours. About 200 nurses attended. Although she was the only woman to die in this fashion, a fair number of men died 'back home' in hospital, often of pneumonia.

A feature of the War Memorial is the sailor, yet Londonderry is not a particularly seafaring place. There was a lively coastal trade to and from the Clyde and the Ayrshire coalfield and, for a while, a shipbuilding yard. Transatlantic liners would anchor off Moville, in Lough Foyle, while passengers – mainly emigrants from Donegal – were brought down from Derry in tenders. So there are only 17 in the *Diary* who could be thought of as sailors – but they are an interesting bunch.

Those who died at sea were not necessarily combatants – in fact, three were in the Mercantile Marine Reserve. Dr William Algeo was the Ship's surgeon on the ss *California*. Sub-Lieutenant McNee was Engineer on HM Water Tank 'Progress' and went down with his ship in the North Sea. Fireman Andrew Anderson was accidentally drowned at Glasgow. First Class Stoker George Gallagher was killed in action at the Battle of Jutland. Able Seaman Charles Trainor (at 44, old for such a rank) died at Londonderry City Infirmary. One wonders how he came to end his days there.

At least one of the sailors died a hero's death. Louis Allen Cattley was the Marconi (Wireless) Operator on the ss *Geo* and was lost at sea. The transport vessel left Messina, Sicily and after about an hour at sea, a periscope was sighted. The transport gunner fired and, at the same time, the vessel was torpedoed. Cattley remained at his post, sending out an SOS. The signals were taken up by another vessel some distance away.

Cattley was at his post when the transport went down. The vessel which got his signals arrived an hour later and rescued 15 of the crew, who had jumped overboard while Cattley lost his own life. His self-sacrificing devotion to duty saved 15 of his comrades.

Fig 12 Diamond War Memorial – the Sailor
Walter M Stephen

I could be accused of treating this chapter as an intellectual exercise, with dead-pan reporting and no emotion. My mother-in-law, Daisy McBride, was one of nine children in the Walker family, pillars of the Waterside in Londonderry. She was born in 1910, and in 1936 married and moved to London and Merseyside (where she endured the Blitz), Worcester, Prestwick and Edinburgh. The worst of The Troubles being over, she and her husband moved back to the Waterside where they found plenty of relatives and friends from their younger days.

In 2008, I was over on the Derry side, saw the *Diary* in Eason's, bought it and hurried back like a schoolboy to share my discovery with Daisy. She was fascinated and we spent hours together going over it. She did not know these people, but she had known their parents, brothers or sisters. She had also read some of their names on the memorial tablet in her church. She had a sad story to tell, which provides some emotional context to conclude the chapter.

One day, one particular day, 30 June 1926, Daisy was visiting Mrs McClay. As she was leaving, Mrs McClay said:

> When you go home could you ask your mother to come down and sit with me tomorrow morning?

Mrs McClay's three sons – Private John 19693, Private Robert 15803 and Private William 24027 – had all been killed on that terrible morning of 1 July 1916.

The Somme is not forgotten in Derry, indeed one sometimes hears a comment such as, 'She's gone up to the Somme'. Somme Park is a fine sheltered housing complex set up by the Royal British Legion Housing Association (Northern Ireland) for veterans and their families. By 1987, it was felt that its original purpose had been served and it was sold to Clanmil Housing Association, an organization with a wider remit.

A small museum of items (dating from the Crimea) contributed by former residents has been kept, to remind us all of the struggles of earlier generations. PLATE 7C. King George and Queen Mary are – rightly – prominent, as are the medals and cap badges of those who served – including a crowned Irish harp.

Derry is one place where 'Their Name Liveth...'

CHAPTER 10

The Scottish National War Memorial

IN THE OLDEN DAYS OF 1946, most factories and offices worked on Saturday mornings. So it was not unusual for my father to be summoned from Glasgow to attend for interviews in Salamander Street, Leith for 10.00am on a Saturday morning. As I said earlier, both of my parents fostered my natural curiosity, did not discourage exploration and provided social opportunities which they thought would do me good.

So I was left on Leith Links for an hour while my father went off to his interview at William Crawford's biscuit factory. Job done (and in the bag), the rest of the day was ours. I had been in Edinburgh before the war, but this was my first real visit. Naturally, like everyone else, we started off with the Castle.

On the Esplanade, there was a fine equestrian statue of Earl Haig, but wasn't there something odd about his sword? There were kilted sentries, a drawbridge and moat, with a splendid gatehouse, with niches (by Sir Robert Lorimer) in which stood our great national heroes, Wallace and Bruce. On we went, seeing Mons Meg and other guns, the wee chapel of St Margaret, our own Crown Jewels and so on, till we came almost to the highest point of the Castle Rock and the Scottish National War Memorial.

Two months before the end of the Great War, in a remarkably prescient statement, the Secretary for Scotland stated that after the war, Edinburgh Castle would no longer be required to house any large body of troops and appointed a committee:

> To consider and report upon the utilisation of Edinburgh Castle for the purposes of a Scottish National War Memorial.

Their report recommended the construction of:

> A dedicated building or shrine erected on the apex of the Castle Rock, practically on the spot on which stood the ancient church built by King David 1.

Robert Lorimer (latterly Sir Robert) (1864–1927) was the committee's architectural adviser. A leading Scots architect before World War 1, he was responsible for many fine conversions and new buildings, successfully balancing Arts and Crafts and traditional Scottish elements. He was involved in the Imperial War Graves Commission and after the war headed up the revival of sculpture by designing many war memorials. We came across his work at Glenelg. Within a few miles of Edinburgh Castle he was responsible for: the Thistle Chapel (pre-war), a memorial communion table, screen and reredos, and the 16th Royal Scots ('McCrae's Battalion') memorial, all in St Giles'. He did the Edinburgh University memorial ('worthy but boring'), the war cemetery at Comely Bank, an altar and reredos for St Mary's Episcopal Cathedral and a memorial for Murrayfield Parish Church. In the 1950s I attended church parades to his St Andrews Garrison Church in Aldershot.

Lorimer produced his own report on the proposed monument and a design which became the basis for what we see now – a museum, a monument and a shrine. PLATE 8A. The old North Barracks of 1755 were embellished on the outside and reconstructed inside to give a Hall of Honour, beyond which is the shrine. Something like 200 artists and craftsmen contributed to the work, making it a participatory effort, and it was only in 1989 that the architect's name was inscribed on the entrance porch.

What did a young lad of 13 find when he entered the National War Memorial? A young lad who had lived through the Second World War and whose grandfather had served in four wars and fought in three, volunteering on 14 April 1915, at the age of 43, for the Post Office Rifles, a kind of 'Pals' Battalion'. His father and four uncles had served in the Army, Navy and Royal Air Force and Uncle Bob had been wounded in the 'Phoney War', patched up and posted to Palestine.

It was more peaceful then. Edinburgh Castle now has over a million visitors a year, and most of them visit the War Memorial. So it is busy, but the visitors are respectful and only one photograph was taken on my recent visit.

The Hall of Honour is lofty, straight and lit by stained glass on the south wall, rather like a cathedral nave. The windows and roundels commemorate 'minor' units, such as the Royal Marines Light Infantry, and portray 'ordinary' life during the war – homecoming at a railway station, a packed troopship, a howitzer gun crew. A giant frieze runs round the tops of a colonnade, with such famous names as Loos, Somme, Gallipoli, Marne. Less familiar names like Piave and Buzancy remind us that this was really a World War, and that Scots did their duty wherever there was trouble.

Facing the Shrine, the north wall has eight recesses for memorials to the senior eight Scottish regiments of the time. Fittingly, in the centre are the Scots Guards and the Royal Scots, the First of Foot, 'Pontius Pilate's Bodyguard'. I remember, as a boy, staring at the latter, marvelling that 35 battalions of Royal Scots had served and trying to imagine how many men that could have been. Even now, I cannot look at numbers like these without a lump in the throat.

Tucked away in the East Bay is the Gordon Highlanders Memorial. Down either side are the battle honours won by the regiment before 1914. Among them are Chitral, Tirah and South Africa to all of which my grandfather contributed. The battering of casualty figures goes on as we learn that 453 officers and 8,509 other ranks from the Gordons gave their lives in the Great War.

Around the Gordons we are reminded of the London Scottish, the Liverpool Scottish, the Tyneside Scottish, the Canadian Scottish, the South African Scottish and the 'Scotsmen of all ranks who fell while serving in English, Irish, and Welsh regiments'.

Also in the East Bay are two splendid plaques to the Royal Artillery and the Royal Engineers. In one, we have gun crews manning heavy artillery while the sappers are building a bridge and communicating via field telephone, signalling lamp and even the bicycle.

Back in the Hall of Honour is the Memorial to the Royal Navy. Under each of these big memorials there is a stone shelf on which are the big red books of the Roll of Honour. Twelve Stephens are in the Naval Roll of Honour, including my father's cousin (whom he never met). George Stephen 3470 was in the Royal Naval Reserve and a Trimmer (one who, on a coal-fired ship, graded and brought the coal to the stokers) on HM Drifter *Beneficent* – a net drifter commandeered and converted for war service. (Curiously, another trimmer on the same ship came from Stephens Close, Braeheads, Fraserburgh). (The Stonehaven War Memorial has him as a Mate. If this proves anything it proves that, in a small ship, there is much multi-tasking.)

The entire crew of nine died at Jutland on 1 June 1916 – a reminder that, around the great battleships, there was a host of ancillary vessels making the sea safe for them. Clearly he and I are impossibly remote from each other, but the thought of him toiling away down below deck in the heat and dust, with all hell let loose somewhere above him, stirs the emotion.

Only one name is singled out in the Memorial. Near the Naval Memorial is a simple bronze medallion inscribed 'Haig 1861–1928'.

Over in the West Bay there are some interesting memorials. The women are not forgotten and ten women's organisations are recognised, with a plaque showing a badly wounded man on a stretcher, with two stretcher-bearers and two gentle nurses caring for him. The inscription reads:

> In honour of all Scotswomen who amid the stress of war sought by their labours sympathy and prayers to obtain for their country the blessings of peace.

Nearby the chaplains have their place, marked by a fine bronze plaque showing a Field Communion in the frontline. A stone plaque entitled 'The Tunnellers' Friends' has two canaries in a cage and three mice. In a coal mine, the death of these little creatures signalled the presence of dangerous gasses to those burrowing under the enemy lines.

The Shrine should be, as it once was, a place for silent contemplation and devotion. Today, there are too many people. Certainly they still behave respectfully enough, but it is difficult to be tranquil and reflective in a crowd – and it only takes one flash photograph to spoil the mood. The bare rock of the highest point of the Castle thrusts through the floor and supports the Stone of Remembrance, inscribed 'Their Name Liveth', which in turn supports a steel casket in which further copies of the Roll of Honour their names are treasured. A painted figure of St Michael hangs from the ceiling and symbolic stained glass fills the windows.

The Hall of Honour records the many units which served in the war but the emphasis in the Shrine is on the effort of the Nation as a whole. Five great panels show the diversity of those who served, marching to Sacrifice and Victory. All sorts are there miners, gunners, sailors, pioneers, kilties led by a piper from the Gordons. For once, a general is up at the front. Some are wearing tropical kit, others gas masks and gas capes. One fellow has snowshoes and a parka. Did we know that there was a North Russia Expeditionary Force? Airmen are there, with a plane, and lurking in the background are the horses that pulled the guns, the camels and other animals. (There is a Trooper of the Scottish Horse attached to the

Imperial Camel Corps and a Sergeant of the Royal Engineers Pigeon Section.) And the women squeeze in at the end of the fifth panel.

Under this frieze is the inscription:

> The souls of the righteous are in the hand of God.
> There shall no evil happen to them.
> They are in peace.
> Others also there are who perished unknown.
> Their sacrifice is not forgotten
> And their names, though lost to us,
> Are written in the Books of God.

The Hall of Honour staggers us with the sheer weight of numbers of those who suffered, while the Shrine pictures for us the diversity and universality of the conflict and gives us reassurance. Whether or not this is justified is a matter of opinion – but there is no doubt that the structure of remembrance is well done. Some might say that the war is sanitised, that not all fought eagerly and died nobly, but what alternative could there be in the 1920s, when the families of the dead had to believe that their losses were in some good cause?

Norah Geddes's True Story began with her looking over the Castle Esplanade to the Castle, with its romantic silhouette and history, and concluded with her poem anent the Scottish National War Memorial. I repeat it here in the expectation that it will now mean more to us, having made a kind of pilgrimage on paper.

The Edinburgh Castle War Memorial

Grey looms the castle's battlemented line,
Enclosing memory's jeweled shrine.
Its pilgrims climb the cobbled street,
Some sore at heart, and dragging weary feet.

Were they but here to see these same grey walls
When dawn's red glow upon them falls;
Whose mass all lapis-lazuli,
Is set against a lucent turquoise sky.

By mist invested, see the turrets proud
Rise from the haar's beleaguering cloud:
Or silhouetted 'gainst the flare
By night, in thunderstorm's fierce blare.

From sorrow, weary souls can find reprieve
In loveliness that changes morn and eve:
Can shed some clinging weight of grief or age
And find the peace that's won by pilgrimage.

And so it was in the memorial shrine;
Carved stone, stained glass, rich bronze of rare design
Show deeds wherein their valiant sons took part,
Whom God caught up and gathered to His heart.

CHAPTER 11

'God bless the Kaiser!'

ONE OF THE most conspicuous war memorials, and one of the most poignant, sits on a hill just outside Stonehaven (Stanehive or Stoney). PLATE 8B. It is a columned circular stone structure, not quite finished, representing the unfinished lives of those who died and is a landmark for miles for travellers on trains running to and from Aberdeen on the East Coast line. Around the top are the 'battle honours', including Jutland. Inside, in the long list of those who died, are two Stephens, one of whom was my father's cousin, who was one of the 6,784 who died in the battle of Jutland.

Jutland was the only major naval battle of the Great War (31 May–1 June 1916). The arms race to ensure that the British fleet was bigger than any other had been one of the sources of tension in the run-up to the war, but the big ships were almost too valuable to risk and it was well into the war before a German squadron lured Vice Admiral Sir David Beatty's battlecruiser squadron into the path of the main German High Seas Fleet – with disastrous results. (Beatty famously said – 'There's something wrong with our bloody ships today!') The British Grand Fleet caught up but overnight the Germans broke away and returned to port. Both sides could – and did – claim victory. The Germans sunk more ships and killed more than twice as many sailors, but their capital ships rarely left port afterwards and Britain retained her command of the seas. Both sides showed courage. The British won four VCs (including the Boy Cornwell, who posthumously became a cult figure) and two Germans were awarded their highest honour 'Pour le Mérite'.

Many of us will have been sickened by the repeated accounts of carnage during the Great War, of which the first day of the Somme is only the most spectacular. But the war at sea had the most appalling instances of the almost total wiping out of a large body of men. For example, at Jutland, according to The Pageant of the Century of 1933:

> HMS Invincible engaged with the Derfflinger, was struck amidships by a 12-inch shell. This ignited the magazines of the two midship turrets, containing 50 tons of cordite and broke the ship in half. Only six were saved from a complement of 1031.

Over 1,000 men sent to a watery grave in minutes, and the terrible irony was that their ship was named the *Invincible*!

The Stephens were fishermen from the Frisian coast who were brought over to kick-start a profitable fishing economy by the Aberdeenshire lairds in the early 17th century. They were settled east of Fraserburgh, at Cairnbulg and Inverallochy, and were modestly successful to the extent that their numbers increased and they spread southwards along the North Sea coast. From the little harbours between Aberdeen and Stonehaven, Stephen families scraped a modest living. The women – literally – supported their men by carrying them out to the boats, keeping them dry as these little creeks had no piers. On the mens' return the women gutted the catch, loaded the fish into creels and carried them into Aberdeen for sale. And, between the tides, they baited the lines and did all the household tasks.

In the late 19th century this all changed. Sail gave way to steam and herring drifters and steam trawlers scoured the seas in search of a catch. There was refrigeration and other improvements in processing. Above all, railways brought the fishing ports into a close and reliable link with markets in the big towns and cities.

A whole new suburb of Aberdeen grew up on the south side of the Dee and harbour, populated by fishermen and all the ancillary workers dependent on their efforts – including, eventually, two fisheries research stations.

I remember the frantic activity at Aberdeen Joint Station in the late afternoon over at Platform 1 – the nearest to the harbour – where an enormous train of fish wagons was loading up. In the morning the fish had been landed at the fish market, sold and processed in the many 'fish hooses' in Torry, packed into boxes and rushed to the station.

On the dot of 5.00 pm the great train – headed up by an A4 Pacific, the fastest class of steam locomotive in the world – would slide out to start its tumultuous non-stop journey to Billingsgate. Within 24 hours of being landed, Aberdeen fish would be on sale in London shops or on hotel breakfast tables.

The traditional inshore fishery was almost wiped out by this new industrialised industry – and many of the casualties flocked into Torry and started new lives there. My great-grandfather, however, only moved the mile from Cowie to Stonehaven, which was a decent town with a good harbour. There he barely kept alive, as did my grandfather Adam, until Stoney, in its turn, declined as a fishing port.

By the time that the Great War came along Adam Stephen had the 40-foot open yole (fishing boat) *Stephens,* registered as A464. He was a white fisherman Socio-economic Class 1 – because he was self-employed – but barely scraping a living. He and his wife lived in two rooms on the Shorehead, which they shared with their seven children. I have seen a photo of my grandmother with a Mr Palmer, who used to lodge with them in the summer. No-one ever told me what the sleeping arrangements were.

As well as the usual mothering and housekeeping duties, my grand-mother was a key partner in the fishing enterprise. When her husband was out fishing, she would fetch up from the harbour a bag of mussels (from Musselburgh, of course) which had been kept alive in the water. She shelled the mussels and then proceeded to bait the lines for the next day's fishing. Attached to the line were leaders and on these were hooks. To each was attached a mussel, tied on by wool. Then the baited hooks were laid round the edges of a large creel in such a way that the line could be paid out safely at the fishing ground, where Adam would pull out yester-day's line, with the catch, and lay down the new line. Line fishing could not compete on price with the big boys from the big ports – but the catch was of good quality.

When the war came, German light raiders and torpedo boats (they had 61 at the battle) made life difficult for the fishing fleets but the white fishermen did not go so far out and were able to keep on fishing most of the time. Many fishermen were reservists and many of the bigger boats were commandeered – like HM Drifter *Beneficent* – to serve as auxiliaries to the fleet. And, as the war went on and the submarine war cut off our food supplies, the price of fish went up. So economic collapse was staved off till my grandmother died (predictably) of a heart attack in 1936 and Adam had to give up the fishing.

Around 1948 my father and I, in winter time, would sally forth about 8.00 pm for an hour's walk, during which my father would practise his recitations of long poems like 'Tam O'Shanter' or Robert Service's ballads. Sometimes he would reminisce about growing up in Stonehaven in the 1920s, when I learned about the town's decline and the disappearance of its seven modest industries, or the Chapel schoolie and the forceful Dean who ran it, or Jack Short (father of Jimmy Logan and Annie Ross), who headed up the summer show down by the new open-air pool.

One evening's thoughts about the fishing brought up the following quote from an old fishwife – not my grandmother.

'God bless the Kaiser who sent us all the pounds!'

Food for thought there.

CHAPTER 12

Andra and the Field-Marshal

ANDREW KIRKALDY (hereinafter known as Andra) is usually considered to have been the best of the old golfers not to have won the Open Championship. In 1860, golf was an esoteric game which was mainly confined to the coastal links of Ayrshire and the East Coast. Of the 35 golf clubs in Britain all but two were in Scotland. The early Open Championships rotated between Prestwick, Musselburgh and St Andrews. The first Open in 1860 was won by a Musselburgh man, (Old) Willie Park, who won it four times and was followed by the other Musselburgh men, Mungo Park (1874), Bob Ferguson (three times), David Brown (1886), and Willie Park Junior (1887 and 1889). From St Andrews came Old Tom Morris (four times), his son, Young Tom Morris (four times before his tragic death at 24) and a string of others – including Hugh Kirkaldy (1891), Andra's younger brother, whom Andra considered 'the best golfer of his day', but who died of tuberculosis at 29. (Andra's older brother taught the Prince of Wales, later Edward VII and the Grand Duke Michael of Russia, who was Czar Michael II of Russia for 30 hours in 1917).

These, and a generation of others, carried the message abroad, but it was 30 years before an Englishman won the Open, and 1907 before the first golfer from outside the British Isles won the Open. Arnaud Massey (1877–1951) was an interesting character. A French Basque, he came to North Berwick at 21, married a North Berwick girl, shuttled between La Boulou, Versailles and successive Opens, where he was never out of the top 20 for 20 years. In 1907, the press said: 'He was a Frenchman with the soul of a Scot', and he was reported as saying:

Me Scotch. Me married a Scotch wife. Me very pleased me won. No Englishman won.

He was wounded at Verdun in the Great War.

For 50 years, Kirkaldy was an active professional. In the Open, he was second three times, was in the top three six times and the top ten 14 times. It was said that he was never outstanding as a medal player but was probably the greatest money match player of his time. (His advice to his brother Hugh was 'follow the siller like every wise man'). For the last three years of his life, he voluntarily took on the duty of lowering and raising the flag daily at St Andrews.

Andra was the stereotype of the old school, rough, uncouth, often drunk, but full of picturesquely expressed wisdom about the game. As a character, he was continually quoted and immortalised by the English Varsity writers of the Twenties. Thus, when carrying for the Prince of Wales at St Andrews, he addressed the intrusive camera crews:

> Awa' oot o' here wi' yer magic lanterns. The Prince disnae want ye and I dinna want ye.

Sir Frederick Ponsonby, in his *Recollections of Three Reigns*, reminisced that Andra was brought down from Scotland to play with Edward VII at Windsor, but got drunk and had to be sent back.

Willie Park Junior was the first of a new kind of professional, as technically competent as his elders, but able to conduct himself with modesty and quiet assurance in all situations. He ran a club-making business, designing new clubs and balls, had retail outlets in Manchester, London, New York and Montreal and designed and laid out about 200 golf courses in Britain, the United States and Canada, and continental Europe. His *The Game of Golf* of 1896 was the first book on the subject by a professional golfer and was, like him, serious and authoritative – while Andra's *My Fifty Years of Golf: Memories* (1926) (Told to Craig Foster) is chatty and great fun.

In 1889, the Open was played at Musselburgh on Friday 4 November. Play started at 10.30am and there were 48 entries. (Some competitors who were well behind were offered 25 pence each to retire early – that wouldn't happen today.) At the end of the day Willie and Andra were level on 155, although Andra could have developed a chip on his shoulder as the result of the miraculous intervention of a hat.

Willie had had to get a three at the last hole to equal Andra's score. The notorious Musselburgh crowd behaved badly and were all over the place. Eventually:

> Park played a full shot with his iron from a tee and the ball dropped among the crowd, hitting a spectator's hat. If the ball had not been stopped by that hat, it would have gone through the railings of the racecourse twenty yards past the pin. Park struck the back of the hole with his second shot, and the crowd started to clap, thinking the ball was in. It lay half an inch from the hole.

Exciting stuff – Andra obviously thought the miraculous intervention of a hat had deprived him of victory, while a putt of half an inch ensured a play-off.

Because the Braid Hills course was officially opened on the Sunday, the play-off was delayed till Monday. A crowd of 1,000 were not on their best behaviour, booing Andra's best shots and making putting difficult.

In Andra's words:

> I should still have won, but for a piece of rank stupidity at the Foreman's Hole. I missed an inch putt through playing it with one hand.

The marker asked him if he had tried to putt that shot, for Andra to reply:

> Yes, and if the hole was big enough I'd like to bury myself in it.

Willie Park finished well, his 155 for 36 holes giving him victory by five strokes, the turning point having been Andra's foolish miss at Mrs Foreman's.

After the match an old professional baited Andra as he was looking for solace in liquid form. As he said later:

> By God, I couldna staun that, I grippit him by the arse o' his breeks and chucked him ower ma heid inta the watter...

Field Marshal Douglas Haig, 1st Earl Haig, KT, GCB, OM, GCVO, KCIE, ADC (1861–1928) was the British senior officer during most of World War I and commanded the British Expeditionary Force (BEF) from 1915 to the end of the war. He was commander during the Battle of the Somme (over 400,000 casualties), the Third Battle of Ypres (over 300,000 casualties) and the Hundred Days Offensive, which led to the Armistice in November 1918.

In his time he was praised for his stolid leadership and his funeral became a day of national mourning. His defenders claim that the high casualties suffered were a function of the tactical and strategic realities of the time – and certainly other generals on both sides expended lives just as freely. He ensured that the British forces played an important role in the eventual Allied victory of 1918, with the adoption of new tactics and technologies by the forces under his command. (Critics wryly observe that this transformation took two years to materialise.).

Particularly since the 1960s, Haig became an object of criticism for his leadership during the First World War. Some called him 'Butcher

Haig', and he was regarded as representing the very concept of class-based incompetent commanders, stating that he was unable to grasp modern tactics and technologies.

In his *On the Psychology of Military Incompetence*, Norman Dixon devotes 20 pages to the analysis of Haig. For a start (Dixon says):

> He was conservative, conventional and, in his attitude towards the French, ethnocentric. His diary and dispatches suggest that he was unemotional and totally anti-intraceptive (i.e. not one to reflect upon his own motives). He was manifestly lacking in compassion towards his fellow-men. He was a confirmed believer in the direction of events by supernatural powers (according to research a common correlate of authoritarianism), and reserved to the point of being verbally almost inarticulate.

> Haig also betrayed that triad of traits which, according to contemporary research, defines the obsessive character and is correlated with authoritarianism. He was obstinate, orderly and mean.

He 'felt it was his duty to refrain from visiting the casualty clearing stations because these visits made him physically ill'.

(In my own – peacetime – military service it was my duty, as junior subaltern, to visit the sick from my unit in the Cambridge Military Hospital in Aldershot. I was not very good at it, but it never occurred to me that this job should be done by the General Officer Commanding Southern Command).

Dixon accuses him of 'early intellectual backwardness'. Yet he had three years at Oxford, where he was in the Bullingdon Club – like our present Prime Minister – but failed to graduate because of illness. Another year would have made him overage for admission to Sandhurst, where he was Senior Under-Officer, was awarded the Anson Sword and passed out first in the order of merit. Perhaps the fault lay in the teaching and the curriculum and Haig's total conformity with the views of authority.

And so to Chapter I of *My Fifty Years of Golf* – 'Celebrities I Have Met'. Andra had played golf with many great men and saw no need to compare one great man with another. But he had his likes and preferences and, 'having done some soldiering', the type of man he liked best was 'the Army man'. Thus he plumped for Field-Marshal Earl Haig as 'the greatest man I ever golfed with'. Not because of his skill, but because 'you never saw anybody... enjoy a round of golf more'.

When the great soldier and I played together during his recent visit to St Andrews, I almost forgot who he was at times. He had no airs or stand-offish manners, but talked as freely to me – and mostly in 'braid Scots' – as if we had been equals. In fact, he almost treated me as his superior, as if golf is the greatest thing on earth. And so it is – during the game.

Not long after the Great War, the Field-Marshal came to St Andrews to 'play himself in' as Captain of the Royal and Ancient Golf Club. When Andra heard that this was to happen, he was 'gey excited' but could not write and offer to take him round. But:

> The Field-Marshal had not forgotten the young professional who gave him his first lessons in golf when he was a boy at Clifton Bank School and I was a boy who had 'nae school ava'... and he very soon sent for me.
>
> 'Hello, Andra, I'll be wanting some games with you while I'm here.'
>
> That was the kind of way he greeted me, gripping my hand and asking for my health and the health of my family... You can understand an army of five millions following a man like that. I wish I had been one of them.

'Playing in' can be a terrifying ordeal, with perhaps two thousand spectators crowding around the first fairways, and the local caddies posted at various points (some unflattering to the new Captain) to get the ball – and the reward of a sovereign to return it to the Captain! As Andra says:

> Professionals know how easy it is to make a bad shot with a dozen or more photographers pointing cameras at their heads.

Andra had a few wise words with the Captain, teed up the ball and stepped aside.

> The gallant Captain took two trial swings and then hit the ball as clean as a whistle, with a grand click, into a bunch of caddies near the road. The caddies furthest off in a straight line had a fine, short and sharp struggle for the ball.

Andra had about a fortnight with Earl Haig, playing with him in singles and foursomes.

> Sometimes Lady Haig was my partner against Earl Haig and his brother, General Haig. Her ladyship and I never lost a match in the foursomes, but I cannot say that I have never been beaten by Earl Haig in our singles.

Once, Andra was reckless enough to try and give Haig a stroke a hole. Haig then played remarkably well, holing one iron shot from 80 yards and beating Andra by two and one.

> The Earl never got flurried in the least, or showed any signs of annoyance when the ball lay badly for him.

The first time they played together, they cracked to one another about their boyhood days in St Andrews, and Haig was as much interested in Andra as Andra was in him. Andra quite well remembered him when he attended Clifton Bank School and used to come on the golf links for a lesson. Haig might have been 14 and Andra 16.

> 'How old are you, Andra? The Earl asked me.
>
> 'About two years older than yourself, my lord,' I replied. 'You must be 58 or thereabouts.'

This conversation occurred as they walked to the first tee on the Old Course. Once the game had started, there was little time for conversation.

> Playing the first hole, I put my second shot into the Swilcan Burn, where I had no business to put it. I was a bit lame that day with the rheumatism in my leg.
>
> Seeing my ball in the burn, the Field-Marshal came over to me and said, 'Stop a minute, Andra, and I'll get it out for you. You're an old man, you know.'
>
> 'Only twa year older than you, my lord,' I said, and we both laughed.
>
> The Earl lay flat down on the turf and, leaning over the bank of the burn, he fished out my ball, without waiting for the caddies to do it. What a picture the photographers missed that day! The Commander-in-Chief of the British Army doing a caddie's job for Andrew Kirkaldy! That's what the picture might have been called. It would almost be worth painting.
>
> ...I was sorry when Earl Haig's stay at St Andrews came to an end. Great men come and great men go, but I, a very ordinary mortal, stop on from one year's end to another.

Andra's is clearly not a Sad Story, and it may be out of place here. But it is worth noting as a parallel to all the other True but Sad Stories we have covered – and as an alternative view of Haig, in many ways the scapegoat for all the pain of the Great War. His critics list his character defects, yet Andra describes a man with the common touch who could abandon self-importance. How could he be so relaxed with a million lives on his conscience? Are all the military experts and historians wrong?

The young Mary, Queen of Scots was energetic, as well as being beautiful and talented. Her outdoor activities included hunting, riding and going for long walks. At Holyroodhouse she and her ladies had archery contests and played pall-mall. A week after the murder of her husband, Darnley, she went to Seton, east of Edinburgh, where she spent 'three recuperative days'. She played golf on the sands (and there is a 19th century painting to prove it!) for which she earned the obloquy of the Scots ministers, who saw this as another example of her callousness and generally loose morals. But it may also have been a demonstration of the therapeutic qualities of golf. Similarly, Siegfried Sassoon commented on the value of the first fairway at Mortonhall to him, during his stay at Craiglockhart.

In the olden days of 1941, when my father was away at the war, my mother, to break the monotony of the domestic life, would take me 'exploring', using Glasgow's superb tram system. One day we took the tram to Dalmuir West – west of Clydebank – and climbed the hill to the public park, where we sat and ate our sandwiches. Looking south, over the Clyde, I saw a complex of newish buildings surrounded by trees and enquired what these might be.

> Oh, that's the Erskine Hospital. There are men in there who were gassed and mutilated in the Great War and have never been out since.

That made a great impression on me.

At the same time she told me that Lady Haig was so upset at the part her husband had played in the war that she completely lost her wits. As a result, the Lady Haig Poppy Factories were set up to salve her conscience. (This is what I was told. It may or may not be factually accurate – but there's no smoke without fire.)

We have looked together at a few of the myriad Sad but True Stories that might have been told about the Great War. Huge numbers were killed. Great numbers had their bodies broken. Goodness knows how many had their minds broken. And yet, such is the diversity and resilience of human behaviour, many contrived to set all that behind them. For example, a few of the survivors of McCrae's Battalion rejoined the colours in 1939 when they thought their country needed them. Ian Hay, the chronicler of *The First Hundred Thousand,* had been through the hell of

Loos, but also rejoined to serve in the Second World War. At a more modest level, my own grandfather served on the North-West Frontier, in South Africa and on the Western Front. Not being allowed to serve in the Second World War, he joined the Home Guard. After the war, he soldiered on as the hall keeper for the local branch of the Royal British Legion until he was 98.

As well as commemorating those who made the supreme sacrifice in the Great War, we must register admiration for those who were able to come through to remake lives in the troubled years that were to follow.

Bibliographical Note

Alexander, Jack, *McCrae's Battalion: The Story of the 16th Royal Scots.* Mainstream Publishing, Edinburgh and London, 2003.

Crook, J Mordaunt, *The Rise of the Nouveaux Riches.* John Murray, London, 1999.

Dixon, Norman E, *On the Psychology of Military Incompetence.* Jonathan Cape, London, 1976.

Hart, Peter, *Gallipoli.* Profile Books, London, 2013.

Hay, Ian, *The First Hundred Thousand.* Richard Drew Publishing Ltd, Glasgow, 1985 edition.

Laffin, John, *British Butchers and Bunglers of World War One.* Alan Sutton Publishing, Stroud, 1988.

Sassoon, Siegfried, *The Complete Memoirs of George Sherston.* Faber and Faber, London, 1972 edition.

Smith, Charles J, *Historic South Edinburgh.* Charles Skilton Ltd, Edinburgh, 1979.

Wilkinson, Roni, *Pals on the Somme 1916.* Pen and Sword, Barnsley, 2006.

A Vigorous Institution: The Living Legacy of Patrick Geddes

Edited by Walter Stephen
ISBN 978 1905222 88 9 PBK £12.99

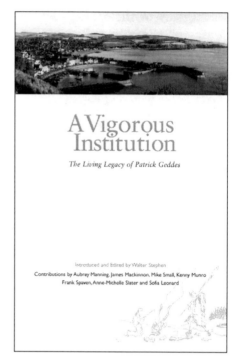

A Vigorous Institution

The Living Legacy of Patrick Geddes

Introduced and Edited by Walter Stephen

Contributions by Aubrey Manning, James Mackinnon, Mike Small, Kenny Munro
Frank Spaven, Anne-Michelle Slater and Sofia Leonard

Patrick Geddes was an original thinker and innovator, an internationalist steeped in Scottishness. His achievements included conservation projects in the Old Town of Edinburgh and in London; community development through greening the urban environment; and town plans for Dunfermline, Cyprus, Tel Aviv and over 50 Indian cities. He pioneered summer schools and self-governing student hostels, used public art to stimulate social change, and established his own College of Art in Edinburgh and a Collège des Écossais in Montpellier.

Aspects of his life are re-examined in an attempt to further understand his thinking. How much of an anarchist was he? How influential were his home and childhood experiences? Why did he change his name and why – till the publication of this book – was his birthplace shrouded in mystery?

Spectacles, Testicles, Fags and Matches: The untold story of the RAF Servicing Commandos in World War Two

Introduced and compiled by Tom Atkinson
ISBN 978-1-906307-85-1 PBK £12.99

Spectacles, testicles, fags and matches was a ritual used by Servicing Commandos after doing anything they called 'hairy'. It was a completely non-religious act, but strangely comforting.

From the jungles of Burma to the foggy plains of Germany, the RAF Servicing Commandos were the men who kept the most advanced aircraft of the RAF flying. Yet there has been very little written about them. Historians, up to today, are surprised to learn of their existence and astonished to learn of their activities. But without those Units the RAF would have had great difficulty in providing close cover for the forward troops and the fighter planes would have spent less time in action.

These elite Units serviced and maintained, re-armed and re-fuelled, repaired and recovered the front line aircraft on which so much depended, and did it all immediately behind the most forward troops. Fully trained in the techniques of Combined Operations they could land from the seas on any hostile territory and establish new airstrips almost instantaneously. Equipped to be highly

Spectacles, testicles, fags and matches

The untold story of the RAF Servicing Commandos in World War Two

Introduced and compiled by
TOM ATKINSON

mobile, and to defend themselves and their airstrips, they would be ready to service the fighter squadrons within minutes, and service them quicker than they had ever been serviced before.

They are, surprisingly, the Forgotten Men. This is their story told by the men themselves.

World in Chains – the impact of nuclear weapons and militarisation from a UK perspective

Angie Zelter
ISBN: 978-1-910021-03-3 RPB £12.99

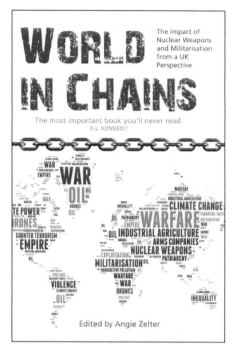

World in Chains is a collection of essays from well-reputed experts in their field, all of which deliver engaging and analytical critiques of nuclear warfare. They point to the changes needed to re-structure society, so that it is based on compassion, co-operation, love and respect for all. Their words inspire us to resist the growing militarisation and corporatisation of our world.

In the past I have often wondered why obviously unethical or inhumane horrors were able to take place, what people were doing at the time to prevent them or what kind of resistance was happening, how many people knew and tried to stop the genocide, slavery, poverty and pollution... I want those who come after my generation to know that, yes, we do know of the dangers of nuclear war, of climate chaos, of environmental destruction. This book will show you that there were many people working to change the structures that keep our world in chains.

ANGIE ZELTER

Details of these and other books published by Luath Press can be found at:
www.luath.co.uk

Luath Press Limited
committed to publishing well written books worth reading

LUATH PRESS takes its name from Robert Burns, whose little collie Luath (*Gael.*, swift or nimble) tripped up Jean Armour at a wedding and gave him the chance to speak to the woman who was to be his wife and the abiding love of his life. Burns called one of 'The Twa Dogs' Luath after Cuchullin's hunting dog in Ossian's *Fingal*. Luath Press was established in 1981 in the heart of Burns country, and now resides a few steps up the road from Burns' first lodgings on Edinburgh's Royal Mile. Luath offers you distinctive writing with a hint of unexpected pleasures.

Most bookshops in the UK, the US, Canada, Australia, New Zealand and parts of Europe either carry our books in stock or can order them for you. To order direct from us, please send a £sterling cheque, postal order, international money order or your credit card details (number, address of cardholder and expiry date) to us at the address below. Please add post and packing as follows: UK – £1.00 per delivery address; overseas surface mail – £2.50 per delivery address; overseas airmail – £3.50 for the first book to each delivery address, plus £1.00 for each additional book by airmail to the same address. If your order is a gift, we will happily enclose your card or message at no extra charge.

Luath Press Limited
543/2 Castlehill
The Royal Mile
Edinburgh EH1 2ND
Scotland

Telephone: 0131 225 4326 (24 hours)
email: sales@luath.co.uk
Website: www.luath.co.uk